# BATTLESTAR GALACTICA ™

# THE MEMORY MACHINE ™

ROGER **McKENZIE**

KLAUS **JANSON**

TOM **DeFALCO**

WALT **SIMONSON**

SAL **BUSCEMA**

BILL **MANTLO**

TITAN BOOKS

# Introduction by
# Richard Hatch

or the past twenty-five years I have been associated with an epic sci-fi series called *Battlestar Galactica*. It's strange to an actor who has starred or guest-starred in hundreds of other more traditional programmes to be best known for something he acted in for only a year. No matter where I've travelled in this world of ours I have always been recognised by those who watched the programme and fell passionately in love with the story and its rag tag fleet of endearing characters. Series and movies come and go but few are immortalised or as fondly remembered as *Battlestar Galactica*. And unlike so many other sci-fi series, *Galactica* reached out to fans of all ages, backgrounds and nationalities. I've been told by many that the strong camaraderie and sense of extended family; the epic search to find Earth and our ancient forefathers the 13th tribe, along with the Mayan, Egyptian and Toltec mythology created a unique mix of heartfelt stories, myth and mystery that touched people profoundly.

It's rare for any movie or series to find the right balance between story, plot, character and action, but *Galactica* managed to do that better than most. And with only one year under our belts it's amazing that we were able to accomplish so much notoriety with so little time to prepare and execute such a breakthrough series that was so theatrical in scope; especially in a day when the technology necessary for translating what amounted to a film as complex in nature as *Star Wars* to a weekly television series was not developed sufficiently. I'm proud of what we accomplished against incredible challenges and feel that had we only had a second year to build more foundation and back-story for the series, in addition to honing our production costs to a more manageable level, we would have been on the air for the next decade as one of the major franchises in television history.

The secret to the success of any series is the chemistry between the characters and a powerful premise that connects to people on a very profound emotional and psychological level. *Galactica* had both of these important elements. The problem in bringing back this series twenty-five years later was the difficulty in assessing the value and future potential of a series that only lasted one year. One-year series are considered failures and mostly forgotten in the annals of TV history. What the executives at Universal failed to recognise is that *Galactica* didn't go off the air due to low ratings but because of high production costs and the inability to film the series in a reasonable timeframe so we could make our airing dates. Well, the truth is you can't keep a good idea down forever and finally, after many attempts and false starts, *Galactica* has made its way back to the TV screen, albeit in a very different way than imagined, although still dramatically and visually impacting.

After much soul searching and having to embrace the reality that a powerful story such as *Battlestar Galactica* can be explored in many viable ways, I have come to appreciate Ron Moore's vision and gifted story-telling, but that doesn't take away from my love for the original series. I believe it's possible to love both the original and re-imagined versions of *Galactica* for different reasons and that it's impossible to compare them without doing an injustice to both. So, I've finally made my peace with where the new *Galactica* series is going and have come to really appreciate the cast, producers and writers of this new show. I even accepted a new role on the series in the character of a Nelson Mandela-style political prisoner/revolutionary. I love playing character roles and the way Ron Moore and staff write makes for delicious, complex and conflicted human beings that are neither black or white and always a joy to play for any actor worth his salt.

After only one season the new re-imagined series is topping the ratings to the surprise of many, but certainly not to many others (myself included), who have always recognised the inherent value of this powerful story. In closing, I'm grateful to have been a part of this epic series and the time I spent filming with my fellow actors and cohorts on the freezing back lot of Universal for many late night shoots will be forever etched in my memory. To my all good friends and fans out there, remember to KEEP THE FAITH!

**Richard Hatch played Captain Apollo in the original TV se**

# BATTLESTAR GALACTICA

™

The memory machine

**BATTLESTAR GALACTICA™: THE MEMORY MACHINE™**
ISBN 1 84023 945 X

Published by Titan Books,
a division of Titan Publishing Group Ltd.
144 Southwark St
London SE1 0UP
UK

This book collects issues #6-13 of *Battlestar Galactica* (vol. 1), originally published in single-issue form by Marvel Comics, USA.

Introduction © Richard Hatch 2005.

A CIP catalogue record for this title is available from the British Library.

First paperback edition: June 2005
2 4 6 8 10 9 7 5 3 1

Printed in Italy.

Other titles of interest now available from Titan Books include:

*Battlestar Galactica: Saga of a Star World* (ISBN: 1 84023 930 1)

*Alien Legion: On the Edge* (ISBN: 1 84023 765 1)
*Alien Legion: Tenants of Hell* (ISBN: 1 84023 811 9)

*Transformers: Dark Star* (ISBN: 1 84023 960 3)
*Transformers: Last Stand* (ISBN: 1 84576 008 5)
*Transformers: Dinobot Hunt* (ISBN: 1 84023 789 9)
*Transformers: Prey* (ISBN: 1 84023 831 3)

What did you think of this book? We love to hear from our readers. Please email us at: readerfeedback@titanemail.com or write to us at the above address. Visit us at www.titanbooks.com

Cover art by **Ungara**

Writers - Roger McKenzie, Bill Mantlo, Tom DeFalco & Walter Simonson
Art - Klaus Janson & Rich Buckler, Sal Buscema, Walter Simonson, Pat Roderick, Barreto & Marcos
Letterers - Jim Novak, Clem Robbins, Ben Sean, Watanabe & John Costanza
Colourists - Carl Gafford, Bob Sharen, Doc Martin & George Roussos
Original series editors - Jim Shooter & Allen Milgrom

**ROGER McKENZIE** has had celebrated runs on *Captain America* and *Daredevil*. In addition to his work for Marvel and DC, he has also written for many smaller comics companies.

**BILL MANTLO** has had a wide-ranging comics career - from stints on *ROM: Space Knight* and *Tarzan* to *The Incredible Hulk*, *The Avengers* and *The Fantastic Four*.

**WALTER SIMONSON** is a veteran comics creator, with a whole host of credits for the entire spectrum of comics publishers - including Marvel, DC, Dark Horse, Valiant, Malibu, CrossGen, Top Cow and Image. He is particularly well known for his legendary runs on *Thor*, *X-Factor*, *The Fantastic Four* and *The Avengers*.

**KLAUS JANSON** is another highly acclaimed comics creator who has worked on a huge list of titles. He is well known as an inker and has inked everything from the *The Avengers* to *X-Men*, as well as the classic *Batman: The Dark Knight Returns*.

**TOM DeFALCO** is a comics industry giant. Formerly editor-in-chief at Marvel Comics, he is responsible for an astonishing body of comics work, including long runs both writing and editing across the entire *Spider-Man* universe.

**SAL BUSCEMA** is a highly respected comics artist who has had a long and illustrious career working on many of the best-selling comics from the last thirty years, including *Spider-Man*, *The Avengers*, *The Fantastic Four*, *Daredevil*, *The Incredible Hulk*, *Thor* and *X-Men*.

There are those who believe life here began out there, far across the universe, with tribes of humans who may have been the forefathers of the Egyptians. Or the Toltecs. Or the Mayans. Some believe there may yet be brothers of man who even now fight to survive somewhere beyond the heavens!

# STAN LEE PRESENTS: BattlestaR GALACTICA ™

BASED ON THE SERIES CREATED By GLEN LARSON

THE PLANET KOBOL LIES DEEP WITHIN A GREAT, TRACKLESS VOID. ANCIENT LEGENDS PROCLAIM IT TO BE THE BIRTHPLACE OF ALL MANKIND.

BUT KOBOL IS LIFELESS NOW. AS LIFELESS AS CAPTAIN APOLLO'S WIFE, **SERINA**, WHO WAS SLAIN BY THE MERCILESS, INHUMAN CYLONS JUST A FEW SHORT HOURS AGO.

NOW, WITH FULL MILITARY HONORS, SHE IS LAID TO REST IN THE BLOOD-RED SUN OF KOBOL...

SHE IS THE LATEST VICTIM OF A THOUSAND-YEAR WAR THAT HAS DRIVEN THE FINAL REMNANTS OF THE HUMAN RACE TO THE STARS IN A DESPERATE QUEST FOR SANCTUARY ON A LOST COLONY KNOWN ONLY AS...EARTH!

## THE MEMORY MACHINE

| ROGER McKENZIE SCRIPT | RICH BUCKLER & KLAUS JANSON ART | JIM NOVAK LETTERING | CARL GAFFORD COLORING | ALLEN MILGROM EDITOR | JIM SHOOTER ED-IN-CHIEF |

ON THE BRIDGE OF THE BATTLESTAR GALACTICA, A TROUBLED COMMANDER ADAMA SHARES HIS SON'S SORROW...

SERINA WAS A FINE WOMAN... SO VERY MUCH LIKE MY OWN BELOVED WIFE, ILYA, WHO WAS ALSO SLAIN BY THE CYLONS.

ILYA, HOW I MISS HER...

COMMANDER, I HATE TO BOTHER YOU NOW... OF ALL TIMES... BUT I MUST REMIND YOU THAT THE CYLONS ARE AWARE OF OUR POSITION.

THE FLEET SHOULD GET UNDERWAY AS SOON AS POSSIBLE...

OF COURSE, COLONEL... I UNDERSTAND...

WHINE WHINE

...BUT SURELY WE CAN SPARE JUST A FEW MORE SECONDS...

...FOR APOLLO...

WHINE

SHHH--!

WHINE

I KNOW HOW YOU FEEL, MUFFEY. I MISS MOMMA, TOO. BUT WE... WE HAVE TO BE BRAVE.

ERF?

W-WARRIORS DON'T CRY...

A FEW MINUTES LATER THE FUNERAL SERVICES END--

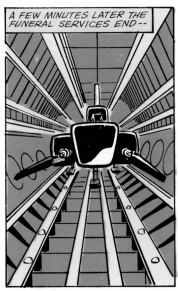

WHHOOSH

--AS AN ELITE HONOR GUARD RETURNS TO THE GALACTICA--

--AND A SOLEMN *BLUE SQUADRON* DISEMBARKS FROM THEIR SLEEK VIPER FIGHTERS...

STARBUCK! WAIT!

STARBUCK! ARE YOU ALL RIGHT?

NO...I DISOBEYED A DIRECT ORDER, ATHENA, AND I PLAYED RIGHT INTO BALTAR'S HANDS!*

IT'S *MY* FAULT SERINA'S DEAD...

*SEE BATTLESTAR GALACTICA #5 FOR DETAILS -- AL.

YOU CAN'T MEAN THAT, STARBUCK!

YOU'RE A WARRIOR... ONE OF THE BEST!

I'M NO WARRIOR, ATHENA...

...A WARRIOR *SAVES* LIVES...

SPAK

BUT EVEN AS A DEJECTED LIEU-
TENANT STARBUCK STORMS OFF
ALONE DOWN A DIMLY LIT CORRIDOR,
THE GALACTICA COMES HARD
APORT...

...LEADING TWO
HUNDRED AND TWENTY
STARSHIPS OF VARIOUS
SIZES AND CONFIG-
URATIONS AWAY
FROM ANCIENT
KOBOL...

...AND EVER DEEPER
INTO AN UNCHARTED
VOID...

AND THE RAGTAG FLEET HAS BARELY MOVED OUT OF SCANNER
RANGE, WHEN, FROM THE **OPPOSITE** DIRECTION, SEVERAL CYLON
FIGHTERS SHRIEK THROUGH THE ETERNAL DARKNESS!

BANKING SHARPLY, THEY
THUNDER DOWN ACROSS THE
SCARRED FACE OF KOBOL, PAST
THE STILL-SMOULDERING RUINS
OF AN AGELESS TEMPLE --
THE TOMB OF THE NINTH, AND
LAST, LORD OF KOBOL --

--TO CIRCLE
LIKE
METALLIC
VULTURES
OVER TWO
FALLEN
CENTURIANS --

--BEFORE FINALLY
LANDING!

OH,
MY!!

BY YOUR
COMMAND,
LUCIFER --

--WE ARE TOO LATE. THE HUMANS HAVE ESCAPED.

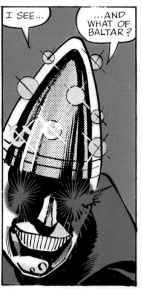

I SEE...

...AND WHAT OF BALTAR?

BY YOUR COMMAND, WE HAVE FOUND BALTAR...IN THE TEMPLE.

OH, MY...SUCH A DEPRESSING PLACE...

...WHY DO HUMANS GLORIFY DEATH SO?

SO IT WOULD SEEM...

...'OLD FRIEND'...

OVER HERE!

L-LUCIFER... ≷KAFF≷... HELP ME... ≷KOFF≷...OLD FRIEND...

...I--I'M DYING...

≷KOFF≷ ≷KOFF≷

I-IN THE NAME...≋KAFF≋... OF ALL THAT'S HOLY... ≋KOFF≋...Y-YOU CAN'T JUST LEAVE ME HERE... ≋KOFF≋...NOT...LIKE THIS...

LUCIFER...≋KOFF≋... LISTEN TO ME! I CAN LEAD YOU... ≋KOFF≋...TO THE HUMANS...

I CAN... HELP YOOOOU≋

OH, MY, YES! YOU WILL HELP ME...FAR MORE THAN YOU COULD HAVE EVER IMAGINED!

WHILE LUCIFER PLOTS, BACK ABOARD THE GALACTICA, LIFE CONTINUES...

...AFTER A FASHION...

APOLLO? LEAVE ME ALONE.

KNOK KNOK

DON'T CON ME, BIG BROTHER! IF YOU REALLY WANTED TO BE ALONE YOU'D BE IN YOUR VIPER, FLYING SOLO PATROL.

WHAT DO YOU WANT, ATHENA?

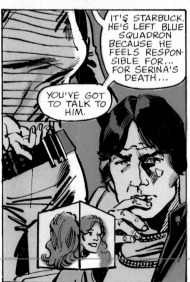

IT'S STARBUCK. HE'S LEFT BLUE SQUADRON BECAUSE HE FEELS RESPONSIBLE FOR...FOR SERINA'S DEATH...

YOU'VE GOT TO TALK TO HIM.

ATHENA, RIGHT NOW I'VE GOT PROBLEMS OF MY OWN--

YOUR PROBLEM...

...IS DECIDING WHICH IS MORE IMPORTANT TO YOU. THE PAST...

...OR THE FUTURE...

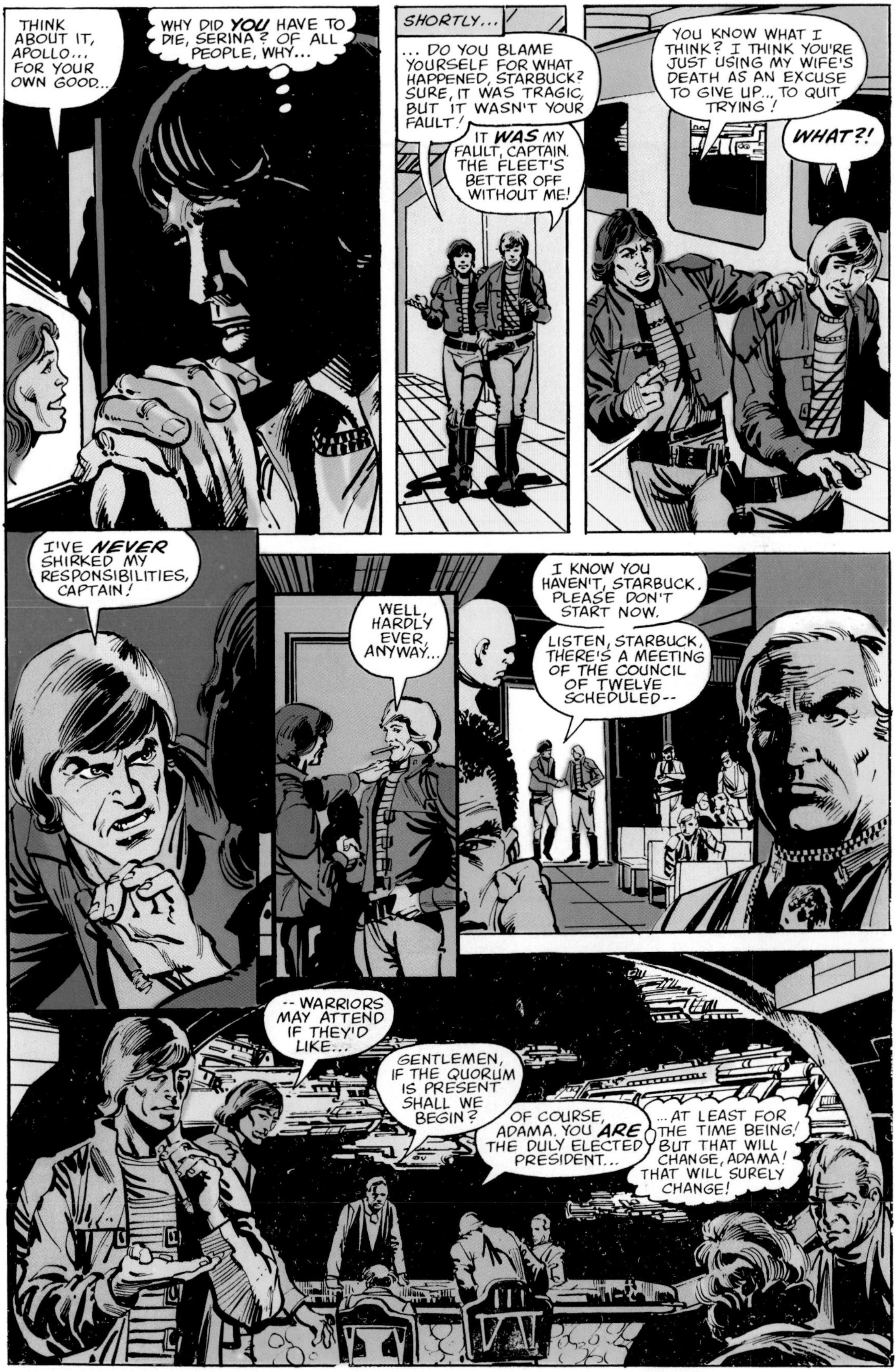
THINK ABOUT IT, APOLLO... FOR YOUR OWN GOOD...
WHY DID YOU HAVE TO DIE, SERINA? OF ALL PEOPLE, WHY...
SHORTLY...
... DO YOU BLAME YOURSELF FOR WHAT HAPPENED, STARBUCK? SURE, IT WAS TRAGIC, BUT IT WASN'T YOUR FAULT!
IT WAS MY FAULT, CAPTAIN. THE FLEET'S BETTER OFF WITHOUT ME!
YOU KNOW WHAT I THINK? I THINK YOU'RE JUST USING MY WIFE'S DEATH AS AN EXCUSE TO GIVE UP... TO QUIT TRYING!
WHAT?!
I'VE NEVER SHIRKED MY RESPONSIBILITIES, CAPTAIN!
WELL, HARDLY EVER, ANYWAY...
I KNOW YOU HAVEN'T, STARBUCK. PLEASE DON'T START NOW.
LISTEN, STARBUCK, THERE'S A MEETING OF THE COUNCIL OF TWELVE SCHEDULED--
-- WARRIORS MAY ATTEND IF THEY'D LIKE...
GENTLEMEN, IF THE QUORUM IS PRESENT SHALL WE BEGIN?
OF COURSE, ADAMA. YOU ARE THE DULY ELECTED PRESIDENT...
...AT LEAST FOR THE TIME BEING! BUT THAT WILL CHANGE, ADAMA! THAT WILL SURELY CHANGE!

MY WARRIOR'S INSIGNIA! APOLLO GAVE IT BACK WHEN WE SHOOK HANDS--!

WELL, I AM PRETTY BUSY RIGHT NOW, BUT... BUT...

... PERHAPS I COULD SPARE A CENTON OR TWO, MISS--?

LIEUTENANT? LIEUTENANT STARBUCK? DO YOU HAVE A MOMENT?

MEDEA. I'VE BEEN LOOKING FOR YOU, STARBUCK. CAN WE TALK?

WELL...

...THERE IS THIS MEETING OF THE COUNCIL OF TWELVE. THEY SIMPLY CAN'T DO A THING WITHOUT ME.

BUT MAYBE...JUST THIS ONCE...

AND I DO HAPPEN TO KNOW OF A QUAINT LITTLE PILOTS' LOUNGE JUST DOWN THE HALL! WE COULD FIND A NICE QUIET CORNER... SIP A LITTLE AMBROSIA...

SOUNDS POSITIVELY SEDUCTIVE!

THE... MOVEMENT... COULD USE A MAN LIKE YOU, STARBUCK.

SO COULD I.

THEN...

WHOA, BOXEY! WHAT'S THE RUSH?

OH, HI, STARBUCK! YOU SEEN MY DAD?

HE'S BUSY RIGHT NOW... AND LET THAT BE A LESSON TO YOU, YOUNG MAN. NEVER MIX BUSINESS...

...WITH PLEASURE!

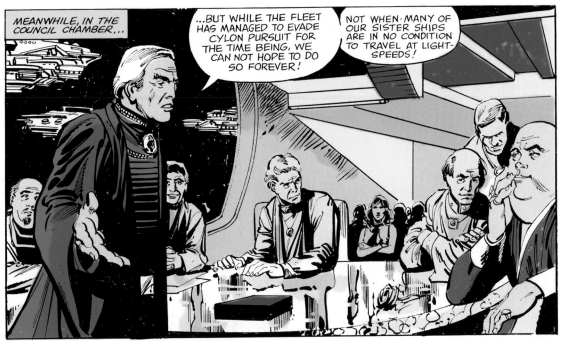

MEANWHILE, IN THE COUNCIL CHAMBER...

...BUT WHILE THE FLEET HAS MANAGED TO EVADE CYLON PURSUIT FOR THE TIME BEING, WE CAN NOT HOPE TO DO SO FOREVER!

NOT WHEN·MANY OF OUR SISTER SHIPS ARE IN NO CONDITION TO TRAVEL AT LIGHT-SPEEDS!

WE MUST DECIDE UPON A COURSE OF ACTION, GENTLEMEN--

--AND WE MUST DECIDE QUICKLY!

AS *I* SEE IT, ADAMA, OUR COURSE IS QUITE CLEAR--

--THE SAFETY OF THE FLEET IS OUR SOLE CONCERN! SLOWER SHIPS WILL SIMPLY HAVE TO BE LEFT BEHIND!

AND WHAT OF THE PEOPLE *ON* THOSE SHIPS, SIRE URI?

WE HAVE NOWHERE ELSE TO PUT THEM!

WOULD YOU LEAVE THEM BEHIND, AS WELL? WHAT YOU SUGGEST IS UNTHINKABLE! BESIDES, THERE IS ANOTHER WAY--

:AHEM:

--ONE I'M SURE MASTER TECHNICIAN SHADRACK CAN EXPLAIN FAR BETTER THAN I!

I'LL TRY, COMMANDER! BUT I'M NO POLITICIAN. I'M A *BUILDER*. GIVE ME ENOUGH VOLUNTEERS WITH QUICK HANDS AND STRONG BACKS AND I'LL HAVE EVERY RUSTPOT IN THE FLEET OPERATIN' AT LIGHT-SPEED WITHIN TWO WEEKS!

URI, YOU HEARD THE MAN...

ADAMA, YOU *CAN'T* BE SERIOUS!

WE DON'T **HAVE** A FEW WEEKS, COMMANDER! WE MAY NOT EVEN HAVE A FEW DAYS!

GENTLEMEN, IN TRYING TO SAVE A FEW MEANINGLESS LIVES, THIS MAN WILL LEAD US **ALL** TO OUR GRAVES--

--JUST AS HE LED US TO NEAR-DISASTER ON CARILLON!* JUST AS HE HAS LED US IN AIMLESS PURSUIT OF A MYTHICAL PLANET THAT EXISTS **SOLELY** IN HIS MIND!

URI, YOUR WORDS PROFANE OUR OLDEST AND MOST CHERISHED BELIEFS! EARTH IS AS **REAL** AS YOU OR I!

I FOUND PROOF OF THAT ON KOBOL-- AN ANCIENT INSCRIPTION** I GLIMPSED BUT BRIEFLY, THAT TOLD OF THE THIRTEENTH COLONY OF MAN! THE LOST TRIBE THAT FOUNDED EARTH!

*BATTLESTAR #3 --AL.

**LAST ISSUE --AL.

THEN SHOW US THIS 'PROOF', ADAMA! LET US JUDGE FOR OUR-SELVES! OTHER-WISE, IN THE INTER-ESTS OF OUR CON-TINUED SURVIVAL, I SHALL BE FORCED TO ASK FOR YOUR **RESIG-NATION!**

YOU WILL HAVE YOUR PROOF, URI... ONE WAY OR ANOTHER...

...AND IT WILL BE OUR SALVATION!

MEDEA, YOU MENTIONED SOME-THING ABOUT A...MOVEMENT... EARLIER. I WAS WONDERING...

WE CAN'T TALK HERE, STARBUCK...

...BUT TWO DAYS FROM NOW SIRE URI WILL BE HOLDING A PRIVATE CELEBRATION ABOARD HIS SHIP, THE RISING STAR.

BE THERE, AS MY PERSONAL ESCORT, AND...

AND--?

AH, HERE YOU ARE, MEDEA! THE COUNCIL HAS ADJOURNED, SHALL WE BE GOING?

OH, FRAK!

I JUST DON'T GET IT!

WHAT COULD SHE POSSIBLY SEE IN A WORM LIKE URI?

IT'S WHAT YOU SEE IN *HER* THAT BOTHERS ME, *LIEUTENANT!*

FORGET HER, YOU TWO! WE'VE GOT OTHER PROBLEMS!

*A SHORT TIME LATER...*

FATHER, YOU CAN'T DO THIS! IT'S TOO DANGEROUS!

I'M AWARE OF THE RISKS, ATHENA!

BUT, FATHER...

...SURELY THERE MUST BE ANOTHER WAY! THIS MACHINE IS A WEAPON OF WAR! A DEVICE USED TO PRY OPEN AND LAY BARE THE MINDS OF TRAITORS AND SABOTEURS! IT CAN BE BRUTAL!

THE MEMORY INDUCER CAN ALSO BE A FORCE FOR GOOD, APOLLO!

IF USED CORRECTLY, IT WILL ENABLE ME TO REMEMBER IN EVERY DETAIL THE ANCIENT WRITINGS I SAW SO FLEETINGLY ON KOBOL! IT IS OUR ONLY HOPE, NOW, OF EVER FINDING EARTH!

BUT IF ANYTHING SHOULD GO WRONG WE COULD LOSE YOU FOREVER! IT JUST ISN'T WORTH IT!

IF IT BRINGS US ONE CENTON NEARER THE END OF OUR DESPERATE QUEST, ATHENA--

-- IT IS WORTH *ANY* PRICE THAT I MAY HAVE TO PAY!

COMMANDER, THERE'S STILL TIME FOR YOU TO RECONSIDER--

OLD FRIEND, THE ONE THING WE *DO NOT* HAVE, IS TIME!

COMMANDER, THIS IS DOCTOR SPANG. CAN YOU HEAR ME?

LOUD AND CLEAR, DOCTOR. GLAD TO HAVE YOU WITH ME.

TELL ME HOW YOU FEEL.

I FEEL... WELL... ...CALM...

GOOD. NOW I WANT YOU TO THINK BACK. JUST LET YOUR MIND DRIFT FREE. I WANT YOU TO REMEMBER.

YES... I DO REMEMBER...

APOLLO, I DON'T LIKE THIS!

IT WAS FATHER'S CHOICE, ATHENA. HE KNOWS WHAT HE'S DOING.

I PRAY YOU ARE RIGHT, SON. I'VE SEEN WHAT THE MEMORY MACHINE CAN DO TO A MAN.

IT ISN'T A PRETTY SIGHT...

LOOK!

A CYLON FIGHTER! IT'S BEGUN! WE'RE ACTUALLY SEEING THE COMMANDER'S THOUGHTS!

THE IMAGE IS FADING... CHANGING... I THINK...

...YES! IT'S OUR HOME ON CAPRICA! FATHER AND I RETURNED THERE ... SHORTLY AFTER THE FIRST CYLON ATTACK!

HE...HE FOUND MOTHER INSIDE... BUT... IT WAS TOO LATE. THAT WAS THE ONLY TIME I EVER SAW HIM CRY...

THE PAIN OF RELIVING THESE MEMORIES MUST BE PURE TORTURE FOR MY FATHER! PLEASE, COLONEL, YOU'VE GOT TO STOP THIS--*NOW!*

IF WE *DO*, COLONEL, IT'S VERY POSSIBLE THE TRAUMA WOULD SHATTER ADAMA'S MIND ENTIRELY! UNLESS...AND *UNTIL*.. HE FINDS THE *ONE MEMORY* HE'S SEARCHING FOR, THERE'S NOTHING WE CAN DO!

"*UNTIL,*" DOCTOR?

THAT'S THE REAL DANGER HERE, TIGH. SOME PEOPLE FIND THEY PREFER THE PAST. THEY LIVE IN THEIR MEMORIES.

THEY *NEVER* COME BACK...

TWO DAYS LATER...

MASTER-TECH SHADRACK REPORTS REPAIR OPERATIONS UNDER WAY, COLONEL!

VERY GOOD, ATHENA. HAVE BLUE SQUADRON CONTINUE PATROLLING OUR PERIMETERS. IF THE CYLONS SHOULD LOCATE US NOW...

BOOMER, ARE YOU *SURE* ABOUT THAT?

POSITIVE, STARBUCK, I'VE CHECKED TWICE! THERE ARE *SUPPOSED* TO BE TWO-HUNDRED TWENTY SHIPS IN THE FLEET BUT MY SCANERS REGISTER ONLY TWO HUNDRED EIGHTEEN!

DON'T ASK ME HOW, BUT TWO OF OUR SHIPS ARE MISSING!

OK, BOOMER, I'LL RADIO THE NEWS TO COLONEL TIGH--

"--AND I'LL BET YOU A WEEK'S FOOD RATIONS HE'S GONNA BLOW HIS TOP!"

HOW COULD THIS HAVE HAPPENED?

HOW IN THE NAME OF KOBOL COULD TWO OF OUR SHIPS POSSIBLY BE MISSING?

ATHENA, PATCH ME THROUGH TO THE COUNCIL OF TWELVE!

YES, SIR!

COLONEL...SOMETHING'S WRONG... MOST OF THE COUNCIL MEMBERS HAVE GATHERED ABOARD THE 'RISING STAR'--

--CAN'T SEEM TO GET THROUGH TO THEM! THEY SEEM TO HAVE BROKEN OFF ALL COMMUNICATIONS WITH THE GALACTICA!

THE 'RISING STAR'? THAT'S SIRE URI'S VESSEL! ATHENA, I'M GETTING A NASTY FEELING ABOUT THIS!

YOU'D BETTER SUIT UP--

"--AND RENDEZVOUS WITH APOLLO AND BOOMER! I WANT YOU THREE TO FIND OUT JUST WHAT URI'S UP TO!"

FORM ON ME, YOU GUYS! WE'VE GOT A MISSION!

BUT, AS THEY APPROACH THE 'RISING STAR'...

BY ORDER OF SIRE URI, YOU ARE NOT CLEARED FOR LANDING!

I'D SERIOUSLY SUGGEST YOU CLEAR YOUR DOCKING AREA--

BOOMER, WAIT!

--I DON'T TAKE ORDERS FROM SIRE URI!

LOOK OUT!

AND NEITHER DO MY FRIENDS!

THIS SHIP IS OFF-LIMITS TO ALL...*ULP* UN-UNAUTHORIZED PERSONNEL...

OH, I THINK I'VE GOT *ALL* THE AUTHORIZATION I NEED!

MORE THAN ENOUGH TO FIND OUT--

WHAT'S GOING ON HERE, STARBUCK?

HEY! GLAD YOU COULD MAKE IT, BOOMER! GREAT LITTLE PARTY, HUH?

UH...GENTLEMEN...I THINK WE'D BEST CONTINUE OUR DISCUSSION IN MY PRIVATE CHAMBERS...

STARBUCK, WHERE'S SIRE URI?

URI? WHY, HE'S RIGHT OVER...OVER...THERE... HE...

WELL, HE *WAS* THERE --A MOMENT AGO! IS SOMETHING WRONG?

PLENTY!

WE'VE GOT TO FIND HIM!

WE KNOW WHERE HE WENT, DON'T WE, MUFFEY?

YIP

*BOXEY!* WHAT ARE *YOU* DOING HERE?

WELL, *UNCLE* STARBUCK SAID IT WAS ALL RIGHT...

WE'LL DISCUSS *THAT* LATER, SON. NOW WHERE DID URI GO?

THEY GOT ON AN ELEVATOR WITH SOME MEN. THEY WERE TALKING ABOUT GRANDFATHER!

BUT, AFTER BOXEY DIRECTS THEM TOWARD A HEAVILY GUARDED BANK OF ELEVATORS...

THAT'S FAR ENOUGH! THIS IS A RESTRICTED AREA!

I WOULDN'T DO THAT, FRIEND, IF I WERE YOU! I'M A BETTER SHOT THAN I AM A GAMBLER...

...AND, FRANKLY, I'M ONE TERRIFIC GAMBLER, IF YOU CATCH MY DRIFT! NOW, WHERE'S YOUR BOSS?

O-ON THE THIRD LEVEL...GULP...HIS PERSONAL QUARTERS...

LET'S GO!

"UNCLE" STARBUCK?

WELL, CAPTAIN, YOU KNOW HOW IT IS...

AND, AS THE ELEVATOR REACHES THE UPPER LEVELS OF THE 'RISING STAR'...

THIS WAY...AND BE CAREFUL, ALL OF YOU!

I SEE WHAT YOU MEAN, CAPTAIN!

HURRY! JUST AROUND THIS CORNER!

ONE THING'S FOR SURE, PEOPLE--

--WHATEVER URI'S GAME IS, HE'S PLAYING FOR KEEPS!

OR AT LEAST, HIS PRIVATE GUARDS ARE!

MEANWHILE, IN SIRE URI'S SUITE...

--THEN, GENTLEMEN, SINCE WE SEVEN REPRESENT A *QUORUM* OF THE COUNCIL... AND IN VIEW OF THE CURRENT CRISIS--

--I SUGGEST WE PUT THE MATTER TO A VOTE... AT ONCE!

AND, IN THE HALLWAY OUTSIDE...

GET THAT DOOR OPEN, ATHENA! HURRY!

*URI!* WHAT TREACHERY *IS* THIS? YOU HAVE NO RIGHT--

I HAVE *EVERY* RIGHT, LIEUTENANT! THIS IS A DULY CONVENED MEETING OF THE COUNCIL OF TWELVE!

A DULY CONVENED--?! ON *YOUR* SHIP? WITHOUT MY FATHER PRESENT?

I ONLY WISH ADAMA *WERE* HERE TO GUIDE US THROUGH THESE TRYING TIMES, BUT HE IS NOT! AND THERE IS THE SAFETY OF THE FLEET TO BE CONSIDERED...

...YOU SEE, I AM AWARE OF THE MISSING VESSELS--

UNDOUBTEDLY, *YOU* ARRANGED THEIR DISAPPEARENCE AS AN EXCUSE TO STAGE THIS MEETING BEHIND MY FATHER'S BACK!

HOW CAN YOU ACCUSE ME OF SUCH EVIL? I PLEDGE TO DO EVERYTHING IN MY POWER TO LOCATE THE LOST SHIPS!

YOU HAVE MY WORD...

...AS THE *NEWLY* ELECTED PRESIDENT OF THE COUNCIL OF TWELVE!

NEXT: **ALL THINGS PAST AND PRESENT!**

# #6

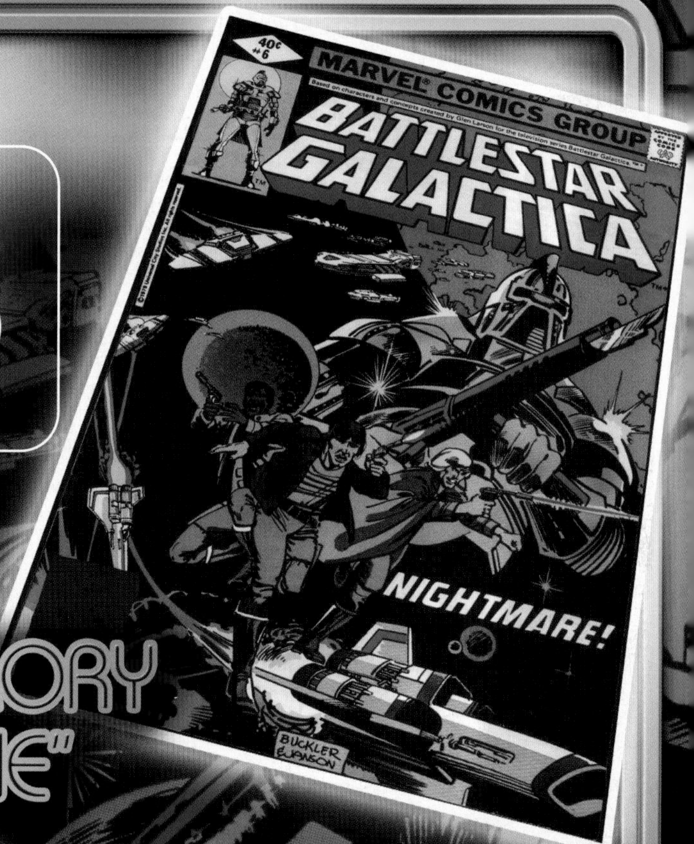
40¢
#6
MARVEL COMICS GROUP
BATTLESTAR GALACTICA
NIGHTMARE!
BUCKLER & JANSON

"THE MEMORY MACHINE"

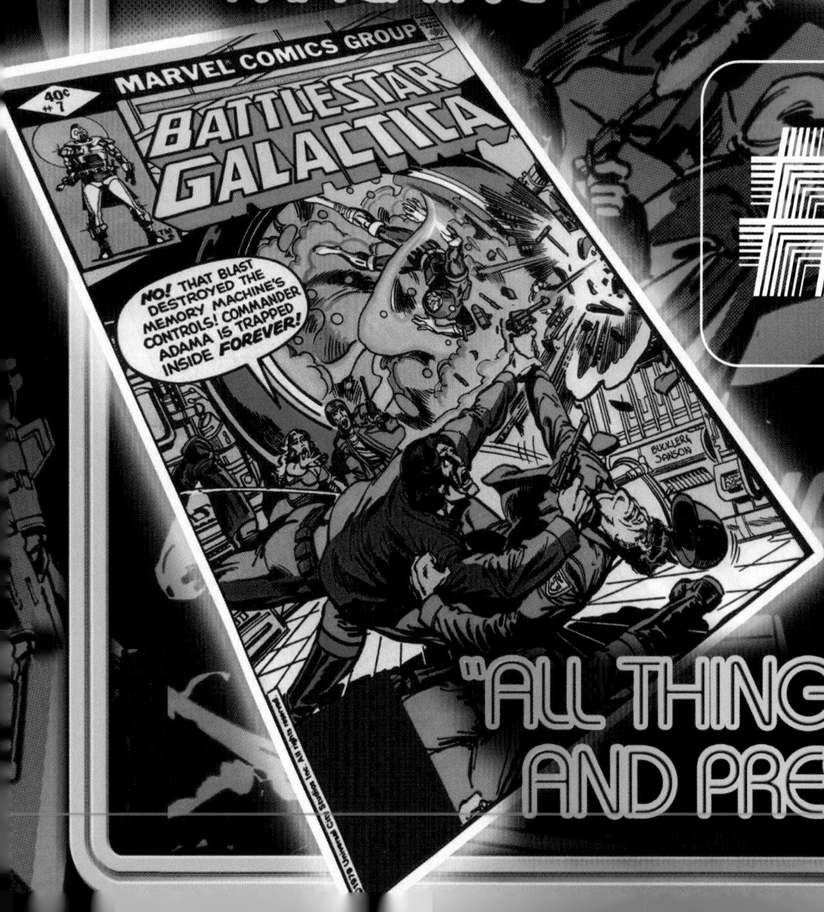
MARVEL COMICS GROUP
40¢
#7
BATTLESTAR GALACTICA
NO! THAT BLAST DESTROYED THE MEMORY MACHINE'S CONTROLS! COMMANDER ADAMA IS TRAPPED INSIDE FOREVER!
BUCKLER & JANSON

# #7

"ALL THINGS PAST AND PRESENT"

There are those who believe life here began out there, far across the universe, with tribes of humans who may have been the forefathers of the Egyptians. Or the Toltecs. Or the Mayans. Some believe there may yet be brothers of man who even now fight to survive somewhere beyond the heavens!

STan Lee PRESENTS: **BattlestaR GALACTICA**

Based on the television series Battlestar Galactica™* written and created by Glen Larson.

| ROGER McKENZIE SCRIPT | RICH BUCKLER KLAUS JANSON | ART | CLEM ROBINS LETTERING | BOB SHAREN COLORING | ALLEN MILGROM • EDITOR JIM SHOOTER • ED-IN-CHIEF |

# ALL THINGS PAST and PRESENT!

HE STILL REMEMBERS ONLY TOO WELL, THAT DAY, SOME TWENTY-FIVE YAHRENS AGO, AT THE COLONIAL FLEET ACADEMY ON CAPRICA...

DO YOU YIELD, BALTAR?

OUR PRACTICE SESSION IS *FAR* FROM OVER, ADAMA! I WILL NOT BOW TO YOU NOW--

...OR EVER!

I'LL BET FIVE CUBITS ON ADAMA!

AND HE REMEMBERS HOW THEIR BIO-SWORDS, ATTUNED AND LINKED TO THEIR INDIVIDUAL NERVOUS SYSTEMS, CRACKLED WITH A COMPUTERIZED HALF-LIFE ALL THEIR OWN... PARRYING AND THRUSTING NEARLY FASTER THAN THE EYE COULD FOLLOW.

A QUARTER OF A CENTURY LATER BALTAR WOULD TURN TRAITOR, BETRAYING THE ENTIRE HUMAN RACE TO THE CYLONS--

--BUT MOSTLY, COMMANDER ADAMA REMEMBERS THAT, EVEN AS A CADET, BALTAR WAS *NOT* A MAN TO BE TRUSTED.

HAVE IT YOUR WAY, THEN.

I *WILL*, ADAMA! I'M A BETTER WARRIOR THAN YOU--

--AND BY ALL THE GODS OF KOBOL, I INTEND TO PROVE IT!

PERHAPS YOU WILL, BALTAR, BUT NOT HERE. NOT TODAY.

OUR MATCH IS ENDED.

RECORDING A STRIKE, ADAMA'S BIO-SWORDS INSTANTLY DEACTIVATE AS PER THEIR COMPUTER PROGRAMMING...

...BALTAR'S WEAPON, HOW-EVER, *DOES NOT*, AND HE QUICKLY PRESSES HIS ILL-GAINED ADVANTAGE

WHA--?!

SOMETHING WRONG, ADAMA?

YOU KNOW FULL WELL WHAT'S WRONG! Y-YOU'VE *TAMPERED* WITH YOUR SWORD'S CONTROLS! THAT IS AGAINST REGULATIONS!

YOU WOULD DO WELL, ADAMA, *NOT* TO ACCUSE ME OF CRIMES WHICH YOU CANNOT VERIFY--

- OR ARE YOU SIMPLY *AFRAID* TO FACE ME, MAN-TO-MAN?

MAN TO MACHINE, YOU MEAN!

BUT IT TAKES MORE THAN TECHNOLOGY--

--TO MAKE A MAN A WARRIOR!

ENOUGH, ADAMA! YOU MAY HAVE WON...THIS TIME...

...BUT THERE WILL SURELY BE OTHER TIMES...

CAPTAIN APOLLO, THIS IS *ALL* VERY INTERESTING, BUT I'M AFRAID IT'S GETTING US NOWHERE.

WORSE, IT IS A FLAGRANT *WASTE* OF THE GALACTICA'S PRECIOUS ENERGY RESOURCES.

THE *MEMORY-STIMULATOR* HAS, I THINK, PROVEN YOUR FATHER'S RECOLLECTIONS OF *HIS PAST* TO BE...AH...DISJOINTED AT BEST.

YOU GOADED HIM INTO THIS, SIRE URI--

--AND WHEN HE WAS IN NO POSITION TO PREVENT IT, YOU *STOLE* THE PRESIDENCY OF THE COUNCIL OF TWELVE FROM HIM!*

I STOLE *NOTHING*, CAPTAIN. THE FLEET NEEDS LEADERSHIP NOW, NOT MEMORIES.

*LAST ISSUE. --AL

WE NEED *HIS* MEMORIES IF WE ARE EVER TO FIND EARTH!

AH, YES, THE ANCIENT INSCRIPTION HE *CLAIMS* TO HAVE GLIMPSED ON KOBOL!*

A LOST TRIBE...A THIRTEENTH COLONY OF MAN SOMEWHERE OUT THERE IN THE STARS! IT *IS* A FASCINATING MYTH--

*BATTLE-STAR GALACTICA #5. --AL.

--BUT, CAPTAIN, WE MUST FACE REALITY, IF ANYTHING SHOULD GO WRONG, ADAMA **COULD** BECOME TRAPPED IN HIS MEMORIES FOREVER.

AND IF **THAT** HAPPENS--

IT **WON'T**, URI!

OF COURSE NOT, MY BOY! OF COURSE NOT!

ALL THINGS CONSIDERED, YOUR FATHER IS IN THE BEST POSSIBLE HANDS.

YOU KNOW WHAT TO DO!

AT YOUR COMMAND, MR. PRESIDENT. BUT WHAT ABOUT APOLLO?

HE WILL BE NO PROBLEM...

MEANWHILE, ON THE BRIDGE OF THE GALACTICA...

COLONEL, MASTER-TECH SHADRACK REPORTS THAT REPAIR WORK IS PROGRESSING AS WELL AS CAN BE EXPECTED.

GOOD. THE SOONER **EVERY** SHIP IN THE FLEET CAN TRAVEL AT LIGHT-SPEED, THE SOONER WE CAN RISK LEAVING THIS INFERNAL VOID!

AND THE SOONER WE CAN DO THAT, THE BETTER I'LL LIKE IT! WE'VE ALREADY LOST TWO SHIPS IN THIS NAVIGATIONAL NIGHTMARE!*

*LAST ISSUE. --AL.

IF THERE'S NOTHING ELSE, COLONEL, I'D LIKE TO SEE MY FATHER--

THAT **WON'T** BE NECESSARY, MY DEAR! ADAMA'S DOING SPLENDIDLY!

URI!? WHAT ARE **YOU** DOING HERE?

WHY, ASSUMING COMMAND OF THE GALACTICA, AS IS MY RIGHT--

--AND MY DUTY...

TIGH, YOU CAN'T ALLOW THIS!

I SEEM TO HAVE LITTLE CHOICE, ATHENA...

YOU HAVE **NONE**, COLONEL.

ONE MOMENT, COLONEL. I DON'T REMEMBER DISMISSING YOU!

YOU DIDN'T, URI, BUT I THOUGHT I'D BETTER CHECK THE AIR PURIFICATION SYSTEM...

...THERE SEEMS TO BE A *SMELL* IN HERE...

COLONEL, I WILL NOT CONDONE INSUBORDINATION ABOARD *MY* SHIP. YOU HAVE BEEN WARNED ONCE. YOU WILL *NOT* BE WARNED AGAIN.

NOW, TELL ME, HAVE THERE BEEN ANY SIGNS OF CYLON PURSUIT?

NONE... COMMANDER. WE OUTMANEUVERED THEM...FOR THE PRESENT...

IT IS THE FUTURE THAT CONCERNS ME. THE CYLONS ARE *NOT* FOOLS. GIVEN TIME, THEY WILL FIND US...EVEN IN THIS VOID!

THE LONGER WE DELAY HERE, THE GREATER OUR CHANCES OF BEING DISCOVERED.

I UNDERSTAND THAT, URI, BUT WE CANNOT PROCEED UNTIL WE HAVE COMPLETED REPAIRS ON THE FLEET'S *SLOWER* CRAFT.

PRECISELY, COLONEL, AND WHILE I HAVE NO DESIRE TO COUNTERMAND ADAMA'S FINAL ORDERS AS FLEET COMMANDER, IT IS OBVIOUS I MUST DO SOMETHING!

THEREFORE, I'M PLACING *YOU* IN CHARGE OF THE REPAIR CREWS...EFFECTIVE AS OF NOW!

URI, YOU CAN'T *BE* SERIOUS--

I'M *DEADLY* SERIOUS, COLONEL. I HAVE GREAT FAITH IN YOU. I'M SURE THAT UNDER YOUR DIRECT SUPERVISION, WORK WILL PROCEED AS QUICKLY AS POSSIBLE!

AND, COLONEL, BEFORE YOU LEAVE THE GALACTICA, WOULD YOU BE SO KIND AS TO INFORM CAPTAIN APOLLO AND HIS YOUNG FRIEND...AH...LIEUTENANT STARBUCK THAT I WISH TO SEE THEM--

--IMMEDIATELY!

AND SO, A FEW MINUTES LATER...

AS YOU KNOW, SEVERAL OF OUR SISTER SHIPS HAVE DISAPPEARED, I WANT YOU THREE TO ORGANIZE A SEARCH PARTY AND *FIND* THEM.

WHY THE CHANGE OF HEART, URI? WORRYING ABOUT THE WELFARE OF OTHERS ISN'T EXACTLY YOUR STRONG SUIT.

STARBUCK'S RIGHT.

NOT A CENTON AGO, YOU URGED THE COUNCIL TO ABANDON *ALL* THE SUB-LIGHT SHIPS--

--INCLUDING THE TWO THAT ARE MISSING!

AND A CENTON AGO THE *SAFETY* OF THE *ENTIRE* FLEET WAS NOT NOT MY SOLE CONCERN!

THINGS ARE *DIFFERENT* NOW!

PLEASE DO NOT FIGHT ME ON THIS, MY CHILDREN. I ONLY WANT TO DO WHAT I AM SURE ADAMA WOULD DO...

...WERE HE ABLE...

AND DON'T WORRY, I WILL *PERSONALLY* ATTEND TO HIM WHILE YOU'RE GONE!

LATER, IN THE PILOTS' READY-ROOM...

I DON'T TRUST HIM, APOLLO. I'D SOONER DEAL TWO-HANDED PYRAMID TO A CYLON.

WE'VE GOT TO DO SOMETHING! WE CAN'T LEAVE FATHER ALONE, NOT EVEN FOR A MINUTE!

I THOUGHT OF THAT, ATHENA. *BOOMER'S* GUARDING HIM!

HEY, WHAT'S THE TROUBLE?

I HATE TO SAY IT, APOLLO, BUT THAT VOICE SOUNDS AWFULLY *FAMILIAR!*

THEY SAID YOU WANTED TO SEE ME!

WHO SAID, BOOMER? WHAT ARE YOU TALKING ABOUT?

URI'S GUARDS! THEY TOLD ME IT WAS SOME SORT OF *EMERGENCY!*

URI'S GUARDS? THEN WHO'S WITH MY FATHER?

THEY ARE...

STARBUCK! APOLLO! LET'S MOVE!

YOU KNOW WHAT TO DO!

SURE THING, OLD BUD--

--UH... CAPTAIN!

WITHIN SECONDS...

FORM ON ME, BLUE PATROL, AND STICK CLOSE--

---THERE MAY BE TROUBLE!

NOTHING WE CAN'T HANDLE... RIGHT, CAPTAIN APOLLO?

THE VIPERS ARE LAUNCHED, LOVER!

EXCELLENT, MEDEA! EXCELLENT! BUT I'VE TOLD YOU, WHEN WE ARE ON THE BRIDGE, YOU ARE TO ADDRESS ME AS--

FELGERCARB--! THERE'S SOME SORT OF DISTURBANCE... INTERNAL SECURITY IS CHECKING ON IT, NOW!

IF I'M WRONG ABOUT THIS, URI WILL NAIL MY HIDE TO THE WALL!

HE'LL GET BOOMER, TOO, FOR SUBSTITUTING FOR ME IN THAT VIPER PATROL.

BUT IF I'M RIGHT, FATHER'S IN TERRIBLE--

--DANGER!?

THAT'S FAR ENOUGH, CAPTAIN! YOU'RE UNDER ARREST--

--BY ORDERS OF COMMANDER URI!

HALT!

WELL, I'M *NOT* WRONG...

...BUT THIS IS ONE MIGHTY ROUGH WAY TO FIND THAT OUT!

FATHER'S HELPLESS SO LONG AS HE'S IN THE MEMORY STIMULATOR! I'VE GOT TO GET TO HIM BEFORE...

...UH, OH...

KRAKK

LET'S TAKE HIM TO SIRE URI!

LATER, AS APOLLO REGAINS CONSCIOUSNESS...

CAPTAIN, YOU ARE IN A GREAT DEAL OF TROUBLE!

OHHH--! I--I'M IN TROUBLE? WHAT ABOUT YOU? WHEN THE COUNCIL LEARNS--

--LEARNS WHAT, APOLLO? THAT YOU DELIBERATELY DISOBEYED A DIRECT ORDER? THAT YOU ARE A TRAITOR?

I'M NO TRAITOR, URI--

--BUT I AM THE CLOSEST MAN TO ONE!

ENOUGH, CAPTAIN! I WILL NOT TOLERATE YOUR SLANDER! BUT I WILL SEE YOU COURTMARTIALED!

YOU AND YOUR TREACHEROUS FRIENDS WILL SPEND THE REST OF YOUR DAYS ON THE PRISON BARGE! YOU HAVE MY WORD AS COMMANDER ON THAT!

SMAK

Y-YOUR WORD AS A THIEF AND MURDERER, YOU MEAN!

LOV--COMMANDER, SOMETHING'S WRONG! IT SEEMS OUR AGRO SHIP IS MISSING!

WHAT?! ARE YOU SURE, MEDEA?

POSITIVE, COMMANDER, BUT--

EXCELLENT TIMING, MY DEAR. APOLLO HAS PLAYED RIGHT INTO OUR HANDS.

BUT YOU DON'T UNDER-STAND--

DON'T WORRY, I WILL HANDLE THIS.

BUT URI, I'M TRYING TO TELL YOU--

YOU NEEDN'T BOTHER, MY DEAR. IT IS PAINFULLY OBVIOUS WHAT HAS HAPPENED HERE.

APOLLO'S TREASONOUS ACCOMPLICES HAVE COMMANDEERED THE FLEET'S SOLE SUPPLY OF FOOD, HOPING TO FORCE MY RESIGNATION...

...BUT IT WILL NOT WORK, CAPTAIN. IF I CANNOT TRUST MY OWN WARRIORS, I WILL HAVE TO TAKE MATTERS INTO MY OWN HANDS!

MEDEA, INSTRUCT THE FLEET TO REMAIN HERE AND CONTINUE REPAIRS. THE GALACTICA WILL *RETURN* FOR THEM ONCE WE HAVE...AH...FOUND THE MISSING SHIP!

THIS GOES *BEYOND* TREASON APOLLO--

THIS IS OUTRIGHT MUTINY AND--

URI, LISTEN TO ME! THE AGRO SHIP REALLY *IS* GONE! IT SIMPLY VANISHED WITHOUT A TRACE--LIKE THE OTHER TWO!

OF COURSE IT DI--

I-IT *DID?!* B-BUT THAT'S IMPOSSIBLE! I NEED THAT VESSEL IN ORDER--

IN ORDER TO LEAVE THE REST OF THE FLEET BEHIND, RIGHT, URI? YOU PLANNED TO RENDEZVOUS WITH THE *"MISSING"* SHIP LATER--

--JUST AS YOU PROBABLY PLANNED AN *"UNFORTUNATE ACCIDENT"* FOR MY FATHER! BUT SOMETHING'S GONE *WRONG*, HASN'T IT? SOMETHING YOU *DIDN'T* PLAN ON! YOU NEED MY FATHER NOW, URI!

B-BY THE GODS OF KOBOL, WHAT HAVE I DONE?

FOLLOW ME, CAPTAIN! AND HURRY--

"WE HAVEN'T MUCH TIME!"

DOCTOR WILKER--!

THERE'S BEEN AN EMERGENCY!

YOU AND NURSE CASSIOPEA ARE TO REPORT TO COMMANDER URI AT ONCE!

WHAT? URI KNOWS WE CAN'T LEAVE ADAMA'S SIDE NOW! NOT WHILE HE IS STILL IN THE MEMORY MACHINE!

IF SOMETHING SHOULD GO WRONG--

EXACTLY.

THOKK

NO! ARE YOU MAD? WHAT DO YOU THINK YOU'RE DOING?

JUST FOLLOWING ORDERS!

POWER OFF
SYSTEMS SHUTDOWN!

BUT BEFORE URI'S PRIVATE GUARDS CAN COMPLETE THEIR SABOTAGE OF THE MEMORY MACHINE...

BRRZZAK

HUH? WHAT THE--

I SUSPECTED URI WOULD TRY SOMETHING LIKE THIS! HE SEEMED AWFULLY ANXIOUS TO GET RID OF ME! SO I WAITED AND I WATCHED--

--AND I WAS RIGHT! DROP YOUR WEAPONS, YOU'RE ALL UNDER ARREST!

OBVIOUSLY HE WAS MISTAKEN! IT'S NOT THE FIRST TIME!

ZZAP

BRAK

GET HIM! WE'RE IN THIS TOO FAR TO BACK OUT NOW!

COLONEL TIGH!

B-BUT URI SAID HE'D BEEN TAKEN CARE OF!

WHEN I GRADUATED FROM THE ACADEMY, I PLEDGED MY LIFE TO THE SERVICE OF THIS FLEET--

--AND I CAN THINK OF NO GREATER SERVICE THAN TO PROTECT THE LIFE OF MY COMMANDER!

NO! ADAMA LED US INTO THIS!

IF HE HAS HIS WAY, WE'LL SPEND OUR LIVES WANDERING THE UNIVERSE IN SEARCH OF A MYTH!

URI HAS PROMISED US A NEW BEGINNING-- AN END TO OUR DESPERATE FLIGHT! HE HAS GUARANTEED US PEACE AND WE BELIEVE HIM!

IT'S NO USE, THEY WON'T LISTEN TO REASON!

URI HAS FILLED THEM SO FULL OF FALSE HOPE, THEY'LL FOLLOW HIM TO HADES AND BACK--

--BUT I WON'T LET THEM DRAG THE REST OF THE FLEET DOWN WITH THEM! WE'VE COME TOO FAR, SUFFERED TOO MUCH, TO HAVE IT END LIKE THIS!

I'VE GOT TO DISARM THEM BEFORE A STRAY SHOT WRECKS ANY OF THIS EQUIPMENT--

--OR ADAMA WILL NEVER ESCAPE THE TRAP OF THE MEMORY MACHINE. HE'LL LOSE HIS MIND TO HIS MEMORIES AND WE'LL LOSE OUR ONLY HOPE OF EVER FINDING EARTH --AND SANCTUARY FROM THE CYLONS!

I'LL KEEP TIGH PINNED DOWN...YOU GO FOR ADAMA! DESTROY THE MEMORY MACHINE AND YOU DESTROY HIM!

IF THEY THINK I'M JUST GOING TO STAND HERE--

--WHILE MY COMMANDER IS HELPLESS...

...THEY'VE GOT ANOTHER THINK-- AND AN ELBOW-- COMING!

KRAK

CASSIOPEA HAS DISTRACTED URI'S GUARDS! THIS COULD BE MY ONLY CHANCE!

SO I'D BETTER MAKE THE MOST OF IT! IF THEY WANT TO KILL ADAMA, THEY'LL HAVE TO KILL ME FIRST--

CRAASH!

--AND I'M **NOT** GOING DOWN WITHOUT A FIGHT!

SPAK

BEFORE I BECAME A NURSE, I CURED MEN'S ILLS AS A SOCIALATOR. AND IF THERE'S ONE THING I KNOW, IT'S HOW TO TAKE CARE OF MYSELF!

THAT'S THE **LAST** OF THEM, CASSIOPEA. THANKS.

IS ADAMA--

HE'S SAFE, COLONEL, AS SAFE AS A MAN CAN BE, INSIDE THE MEMORY MACHINE, BUT, IF NOT FOR YOU--

CASSIOPEA, LISTEN! SOMEONE'S COMING!

MAYBE IT'S BLUE SQUADRON! MAYBE APOLLO AND STARBUCK--

MAYBE--

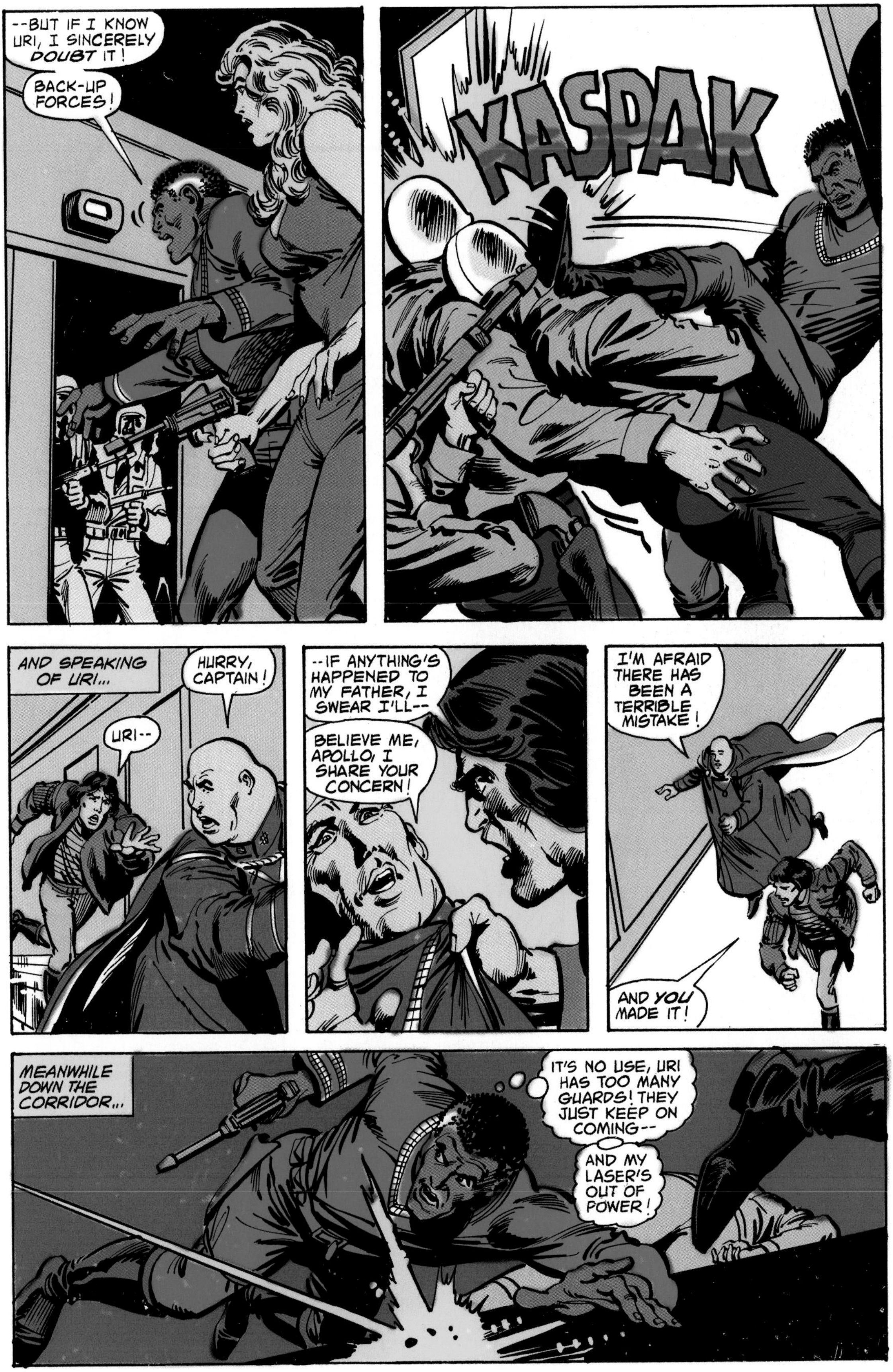
--BUT IF I KNOW URI, I SINCERELY DOUBT IT!
BACK-UP FORCES!
KASPAK
AND SPEAKING OF URI...
HURRY, CAPTAIN!
URI--
--IF ANYTHING'S HAPPENED TO MY FATHER, I SWEAR I'LL--
BELIEVE ME, APOLLO, I SHARE YOUR CONCERN!
I'M AFRAID THERE HAS BEEN A TERRIBLE MISTAKE!
AND YOU MADE IT!
MEANWHILE DOWN THE CORRIDOR...
IT'S NO USE, URI HAS TOO MANY GUARDS! THEY JUST KEEP ON COMING--
AND MY LASER'S OUT OF POWER!

LISTEN TO ME, ALL OF YOU! PUT DOWN YOUR WEAPONS!

THAT'S A DIRECT ORDER!

COLONEL, WE TAKE OUR ORDERS FROM COMMANDER URI--

--AND HIS ORDERS ARE QUITE EXPLICIT! FOR THE GOOD OF THE FLEET, ADAMA MUST BE STOPPED!

IF YOU BELIEVE THAT--

--YOU'RE ALL BIGGER FOOLS THAN I THOUGHT! IF NOT FOR ADAMA'S LEADERSHIP, THERE WOULD *BE* NO FLEET!

YOU CAN'T TURN YOUR BACK ON HIM NOW--

--NOT WHEN HE'S RISKED HIS SANITY... HIS VERY LIFE... TO HELP YOU ALL!

COMMANDER URI HAS SAID WE MUST HELP OURSELVES! WE HAVE TO BE STRONG--

--AND OUR STRENGTH MUST COME FROM LEADERSHIP, NOT DREAMS AND HALF-REMEMBERED FANTASIES!

GO ON, GET THIS OVER WITH! DESTROY THE MEMORY MACHINE!

N-NO! DO SOMETHING, APOLLO! STOP THOSE...THOSE MISGUIDED TRAITORS!

GET AWAY FROM MY FATHER!

DID YOU HEAR ME? I SAID--

BUT THEN, BEFORE AN ENRAGED CAPTAIN APOLLO CAN PREVENT IT--

--A SIZZLING BURST OF LASER FIRE RIPS THROUGH THE COMPUTER CONTROLS OF THE MEMORY MACHINE!

SZZAK!

O-OH, NO--!

CAPTAIN! WHAT HAVE YOU DONE?

THE MEMORY MACHINE IS OUT OF CONTROL! ADAMA'S TRAPPED IN THERE...TRAPPED WITHIN HIS MEMORIES--

--AND THERE'S NOTHING WE CAN DO!

TO BE CONTINUED...

# #8

## "SHUTTLE-DIPLOMACY!"

# #9

## "SPACE MIMIC"

There are those who believe life here began out there, far across the universe, with tribes of humans who may have been the forefathers of the Egyptians. Or the Toltecs. Or the Mayans. Some believe there may yet be brothers of man who even now fight to survive somewhere beyond the heavens!

# STAN LEE PRESENTS: BattlestaR GALACTICA ™ •

Based on the television series Battlestar Galactica™ * written and created by Glen Larson.

BILL MANTLO — WRITER | SAL BUSCEMA & KLAUS JANSON — ARTISTS | C. ROBINS, LETTERS — B. SEAN; COLORS | ALLEN MILGROM — EDITOR | J. SHOOTER — ED-IN-CHIEF

MERE SECONDS AGO, APOLLO, CASSIOPEA AND COLONEL TIGH PREVENTED THE ASSASINATION OF COMMANDER ADAMA BY SIRE URI'S AGENTS!

BUT THE *MEMORY MACHINE* IS DAMAGED!

WITH THE COMMANDER INSIDE IT!

FATHER!

SIRE URI, WHAT ARE YOUR ORDERS?

TIGH, WHAT CAN WE DO?

WE COULD,,, PRAY!

I--I DON'T KNOW! THE FLEET'S IN DANGER,,,

,,,AND ONLY ADAMA CAN SAVE US!

LG516.

AND WHILE THE *BATTLESTAR GALACTICA* LEADS THE FINAL REMNANTS OF MANKIND DEEPER INTO THE STARLESS *VOID*--

--COMMANDER ADAMA DRIFTS THROUGH HIS OWN, PERSONAL PAST, SEARCHING THE BYWAYS OF CONSCIOUSNESS FOR ANOTHER LOOK AT A BRIEFLY-GLIMPSED INSCRIPTION DISCOVERED IN A TOMB ON THE PLANET KOBOL! BUT THE MEMORY MACHINE IS NON-SELECTIVE, AND A MAN MAY REVISIT MEMORIES AND WORLDS HE HAS LONG FORGOTTEN--

# SHUTTLE-DIPLOMACY!

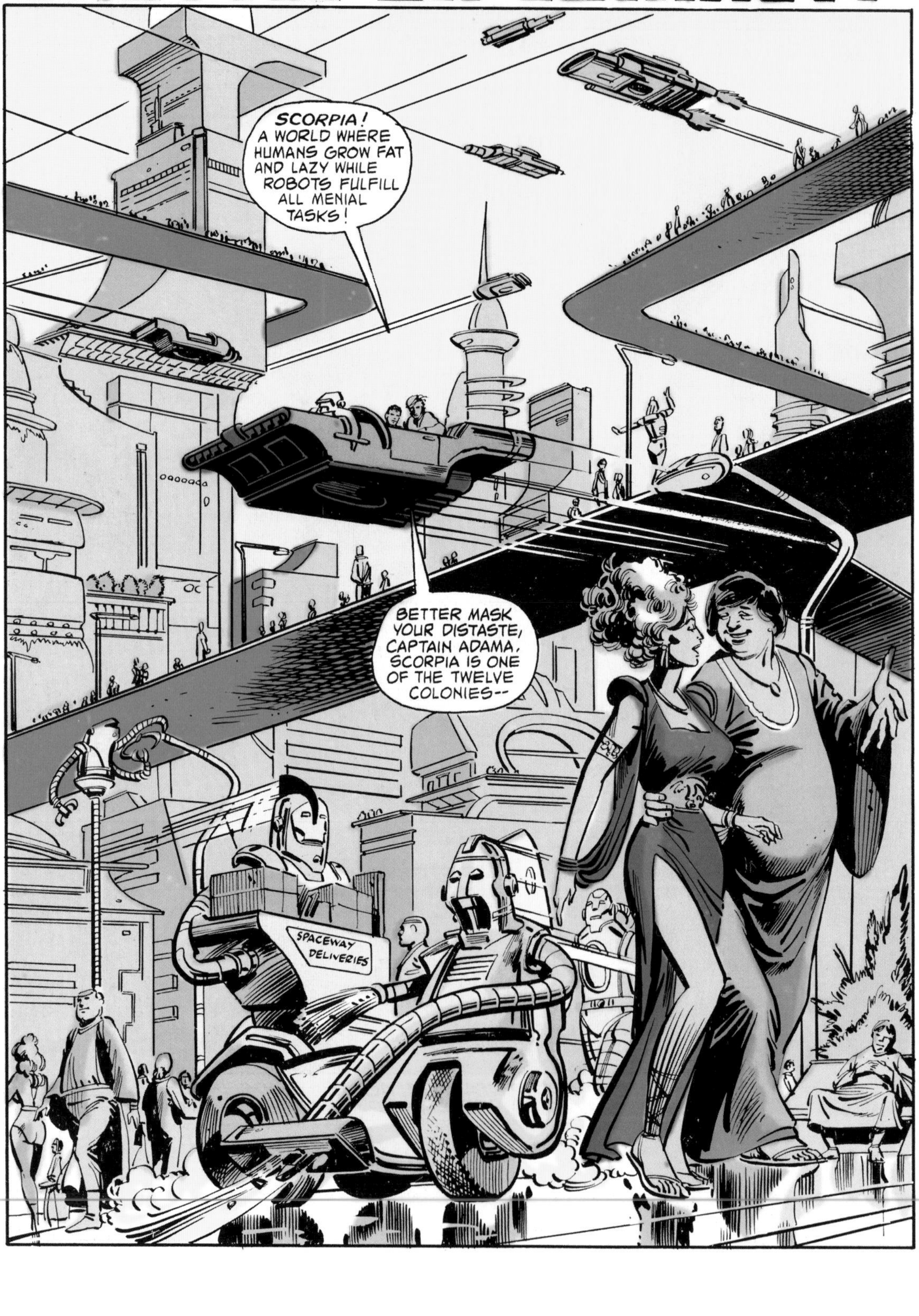
SCORPIA! A WORLD WHERE HUMANS GROW FAT AND LAZY WHILE ROBOTS FULFILL ALL MENIAL TASKS!
BETTER MASK YOUR DISTASTE, CAPTAIN ADAMA. SCORPIA IS ONE OF THE TWELVE COLONIES--
SPACEWAY DELIVERIES

--AND LIKE IT OR NOT, COMMANDER RAYNON STRESSED THE IMPORTANCE OF OUR MISSION BEFORE WE LEFT THE GALACTICA.

I WON'T JEAPORDIZE THE MISSION, LIEUTENANT TIGH... BUT I'M ENTITLED TO MY OPINION.

ON OUR WORLD, CAPRICA, WE SURPRESSED THE RISE OF ROBOTICS BECAUSE WE BELIEVE THERE IS NO SUBSTITUTE FOR HUMAN EFFORT.

STILL, LIKE OUR PILOT-DRONES, SCORPIA SEEMS TO RUN SMOOTHLY.

DOES IT, TIGH? LOOK!

THE SKYWALK! IT'S BUCKLING!

WHY DON'T THE SERVO-DRONES STOP IT?!

FINALLY THE SKYWALK RAMP GRINDS TO A HALT--BUT NOT BEFORE A SCORE OF PEDESTRIANS IS ENDANGERED!

THEY CAN'T HANG ON MUCH LONGER!

SOMEBODY SUMMON THE RESCUE ROBOTS!

HELP! PLEASE, HELP US!

ADAMA, LOOK! HERE COME THE RESCUE-ROBOTS NOW!

BUT THE ROBOTS' WEIGHT IS CAUSING THE SKYWALK TO BUCKLE EVEN FASTER! WE'VE GOT TO HELP! PILOT-DRONE, BRING US CLOSER!

≷NEGATIVE, SIR. MY ORDERS ARE TO CONVEY YOU DIRECTLY TO THE EMBASSY.≷

WHAT--?!

≷THERE ARE BUT TWO LEFT.≷

≷ALERT THE AIR-DRONES··≷

≷--THOUGH THIS UNIT ESTIMATES THEY WILL NOT ARRIVE IN TIME.≷

SOME-BODY HELP US! PLEASE!

ON ALL LEVELS, THE MEN OF SCORPIA STAND ROOTED IN SHOCK.

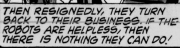

THEN RESIGNEDLY, THEY TURN BACK TO THEIR BUSINESS. IF THE ROBOTS ARE HELPLESS, THEN THERE IS NOTHING THEY CAN DO!

BUT CAPTAIN ADAMA OF THE BATTLESTAR GALAC-TICA REFUSES TO CON-SIGN ANY HUMAN LIFE TO FATE!

TIGH, TAKE COMMAND OF THIS HOVERCAR!

ONE STEP AHEAD OF YOU, CAPTAIN!

SKRAK

≷SKREEE≷

CONTROLS OVERRIDDEN, CAPTAIN--BUT IT'LL TAKE ME A MINUTE TO CHANGE OUR COURSE!

THAT WOMAN AND HER CHILD DON'T HAVE A MINUTE, TIGH!

ADAMA!

COME BACK FOR ME, TIGH! I'M COUNTING ON YOU!

PLEASE-- CAN YOU HELP US?

I'LL...TRY! HOLD THE CHILD TIGHTLY... AND I'LL REACH OUT FOR YOU!

I DON'T INTEND TO! HAVE COURAGE-- THERE ARE RESCUE-DRONES WAITING BELOW!

B-BUT, YOU CAN'T HOLD US FOR- EVER!

I'M GOING TO SWING YOU TOWARDS THEM!

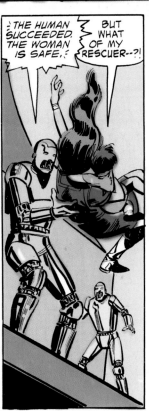

THE HUMAN SUCCEEDED. THE WOMAN IS SAFE.

BUT WHAT OF MY RESCUER--?!

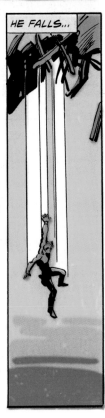

HE FALLS...

TIGH!!

IT TOOK ME LONGER THAN I THOUGHT TO MASTER THE HOVERCAR'S STEERING, ADAMA, SORRY.

BETTER LATE THAN NEVER, OLD FRIEND. THANKS.

HMM, LOOKS LIKE WE'VE GOT AN AIR ESCORT--

--TO DELIVER US TO THE SCORPIAN EMBASSY!

=GREETINGS, GENTLEMEN, THE AMBASSADOR HAS BEEN AWAITING YOUR ARRIVAL MOST ANXIOUSLY.=

ER--YES! WE WERE UNAVOIDABLY DETAINED!

ONCE INSIDE THE SPLENDOROUS EMBASSY...

GODS! ROBOTS EVEN HERE--AT THE VERY HIGHEST LEVELS OF GOVERNMENT!

THE SCORPIANS' WAYS AREN'T OURS, ADAMA.

THERE IS GOING TO COME A DAY WHEN ONLY HUMAN INGE- NUITY CAN SAVE THE HUMAN RACE FROM DISASTER, TIGH!

YET THE SCORPIANS ALLOW THEIR ABILITIES TO ATROPHY WHILE THEIR ROBOTS THINK AND ACT FOR THEM!

GENTLEMEN, WELCOME TO SCORPIA.

THE AMBASSADOR WILL SEE YOU NOW.

CAPTAIN ADAMA, LIEUTENANT TIGH, I AM SCORPIA'S AMBASSADOR TO THE COUNCIL OF TWELVE.

YOUR EXCELLENCY, I BRING YOU THE GREETINGS AND SALUTATIONS OF RANYON, COMMANDER OF THE BATTLESTAR GALACTICA.

THE OTHER AMBASSADORS OF THE TWELVE COLONIES AWAIT YOUR PRESENCE IN ORDER TO SIGN A MUTUAL DEFENSE PACT. ONLY UNITED CAN WE HOPE TO FRUSTRATE THE CYLONS' PLAN OF CONQUEST!

WE HAVE A FIGHTER SQUAD WAITING TO ESCORT YOU--

FIGHTERS? IMPOSSIBLE! I MUST TRAVEL AS BEFITS MY STATION--IN A SCORPIAN *DIPLOMATIC SHUTTLE.*

EXCELLENCY, YOU MUST BE JOKING! SHUTTLES ARE SLOW AND POORLY-ARMED!

THE CYLONS MAY KNOW OF THIS GATHERING! IF THEY ATTACK US--!

THAT IS WHY YO!! TWO GENTLEMEN HAVE BEEN SENT TO PROTECT ME, SCORPIA HAS ONLY ROBOT WARRIORS--

--AND THE PREJUDICES OF THE OTHER COLONIES LED TO THEIR INSISTENCE THAT I TRUST MYSELF TO A HUMAN ESCORT. I DEFER TO THEIR JUDGEMENT--BUT WE WILL GO BY SHUTTLE.

LATER...

THERE SHE IS, CAPTAIN ADAMA-- THE PRIDE AND JOY OF SCORPIA'S DIPLOMATIC FLEET! THE MECH-ROBOTS ARE FITTING HER FOR HER MISSION NOW!

I DON'T SEE THE CREW!

WHY, THE ROBOTS ARE THE CREW AND BATTLE-CONTINGENT AS WELL, CAPTAIN!

ROBOTS?

WE'RE ON A SUPER-SENSITIVE MISSION THROUGH CYLON-INFESTED SPACE--

--AND NOT A SINGLE MEMBER OF MY CREW IS HUMAN??!

OF COURSE NOT! OH, YOU WILL BE SHUTTLING THE AMBASSADOR'S DIPLOMATIC STAFF, THEY'RE HUMAN.

BUT THE ROBOTS ARE SO MUCH BETTER SUITED TO OPERATING A STARSHIP AND FIGHTING THAN... HUMANS.

WHAT MY AIDE MEANS IS THAT THE HUMANS OF SCORPIA CONSIDER FIGHTING AND THE MECHANICS OF SPACE TRAVEL BENEATH THEM, GENTLEMEN.

AND WHAT DO YOU THINK, AMBASSADOR?

I AM MERELY A SERVANT TO MY PLANET, CAPTAIN. LIKE YOU, I DO NOT QUESTION POLICY.

I MERELY CARRY OUT ORDERS.

HOURS LATER, THE SCORPIAN SHUTTLE IS SPACE-BOUND.

I DON'T *LIKE* IT, TIGH! THESE ROBOTS REMIND ME TOO MUCH OF OUR CYLON ENEMIES!

IF I HAD A VOICE ON THE COUNCIL I'D ADVISE AGAINST ALLYING WITH THE SCORPIANS!

IT'S UNFAIR TO ASK THE OTHER ELEVEN COLONIES TO RELY ON A PLANET WHERE HUMANS LET ROBOTS DO THEIR FIGHTING FOR THEM!

IF THE ROBOTS WERE MERELY SERVANTS, I COULD UNDERSTAND IT--

BUT WHAT BOTHERS YOU, GENTLEMEN, IS THAT ON SCORPIO, HUMANS HAVE PRACTICALLY GIVEN THE GOVERNING OF THEIR WORLD OVER TO THEIR MACHINES,

AMBASSADOR--?!

BE AT EASE, CAPTAIN. WHAT YOU HAVE SAID IS TRUE.

THE HUMANS OF MY WORLD HAVE BECOME WEAK, CONTENT TO BE SERVED.

BUT MANKIND MUST FACE THE THREAT OF THE CYLONS COLLECTIVELY. CAN SCORPIA BE ROUSED FROM HER LETHARGY IN TIME --WITHOUT RISKING A VAST SOCIAL UPHEAVAL THAT WOULD TEAR HER APART?

AND WHAT OF THE ROBOTS? THEY HAVE SERVED LONG AND FAITHFULLY. ARE THEY TO BE BLAMED FOR DOING MERELY WHAT THEY WERE CREATED TO DO?

I DON'T--

ADAMA!

CYLONS! WE'VE FLOWN INTO AN *AMBUSH!!*

THE CYLON RAIDERS ARE SILENT, SWIFT, AND DEADLY.

THE SHUTTLE DOES NOT STAND A CHANCE!

UNLESS...

WE CANNOT OUTRUN THEM, CAPTAIN?

NOT A CHANCE, YOUR EXCELLENCY! THEY'VE GOT THE SPEED AND THE FIREPOWER--

--WHILE ALL WE'VE GOT IS HUMAN INGENUITY!

YOU HAVE A PLAN?

YES! YOU SEE THAT SMALL WORLD, AMBASSADOR? IT'S CALLED *VESPER!*

A PEACEFUL-SOUNDING NAME FOR A WORLD RAVAGED BY SAVAGE ASTRALON STORMS!

IF WE CAN MAKE CLOUD-COVER, THEIR SCANNERS WON'T BE ABLE TO GET A FIX ON US!

WE'RE *IN!* NOW, IF THE CYLONS DON'T GET US, THE STORM JUST MIGHT. WE'VE GOT TO TRY AND EVEN THE ODDS!

SHUTTLE'S ARMED WITH A SINGLE TURBO-LASER CANNON!

IT WILL HAVE TO DO!!

SHRAK

IT DOES!

THE BLASTED CYLON RAIDER CAROMS WILDLY INTO ONE OF ITS COMPANION SHIPS.

BUT TWO MORE OPEN FIRE ON THE SHUTTLE!

THE GUNS OF ONE CYLON CRAFT ARE SILENCED BY A SEARING ARC OF ASTRALIGHTNING!

ZSHKROW

SHUTTLE'S DAMAGED, ADAMA! WE'RE GOING TO--

KRASSH!

SILENCE.

THEN, AUTOMATED WARRIOR-DRONES SCRAMBLE FROM THE DISEMBOWELED SHUTTLE!

≶WARRIOR-DRONES FAN OUT, UPWARD SCAN, THE FOE WILL STRIKE FROM THE SKIES.≶

≶HUMANS MUST BE PRO-TECTED. THAT IS THE PRIME DIRECTIVE.≶

THE ROBOTS ARE TAKING UP DEFENSIVE POSITIONS, ADAMA!

WHAT OF THE HUMAN PASSEN-GERS?

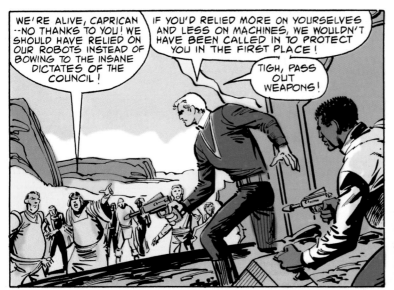

WE'RE ALIVE, CAPRICAN--NO THANKS TO YOU! WE SHOULD HAVE RELIED ON OUR ROBOTS INSTEAD OF BOWING TO THE INSANE DICTATES OF THE COUNCIL!

IF YOU'D RELIED MORE ON YOURSELVES AND LESS ON MACHINES, WE WOULDN'T HAVE BEEN CALLED IN TO PROTECT YOU IN THE FIRST PLACE!

TIGH, PASS OUT WEAPONS!

WE GOT OFF A DISTRESS CALL TO THE GALACTICA BEFORE WE WENT DOWN, BUT THE CYLONS WILL GET HERE ANY MICRON!

WE'VE GOT TO FIGHT THEM OFF TILL HELP ARRIVES!

FIGHT? HOW ABHORRENT!

MAYBE, BUT IT'S A LOT MORE PLEASANT THAN WHAT'LL HAPPEN TO YOU IF YOU SURRENDER TO THE CYLONS!

RUBBISH! WE HAVE THE ROBOTS --AND YOU, OFFWORLDERS--TO UNDERTAKE THE LOWLY TASK OF DEFENDING US!

WHY YOU--!

CEASE YOUR QUARRELING. SCORPIANS, YOU MUST FIGHT BESIDE YOUR ROBOTS--

--OR DIE WITH THEM.

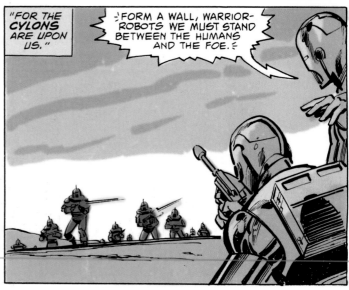

"FOR THE CYLONS ARE UPON US."

~FORM A WALL, WARRIOR-ROBOTS WE MUST STAND BETWEEN THE HUMANS AND THE FOE.~

BUT NO WALL, NO MATTER HOW STRONG, IS, UNBREACHABLE!

:SKREE:

FORWARD, CYLONS!

SEEK COVER! CLIMB!

O-OUR ROBOTS FELL-- MOST OF THEM WERE DESTROYED!

YES, BUT THEY PUT UP A VALIANT FIGHT BEFORE THEIR DEFEAT!

THEY BOUGHT US TIME! LET'S USE IT!

MEANWHILE WE'VE GOT TWO LASER-PISTOLS AGAINST A SCORE OF CYLONS!

I HAVE ONLY ONE SUGGESTION, TIGH...

"...MAKE EVERY SHOT COUNT!"

SHAK

SHRAK

TWO BLASTERS WILL NOT HOLD THEM FOR LONG, CAPTAIN ADAMA. MAY I HAVE A LASER PISTOL?

I THOUGHT YOU SCORPIANS LET YOUR ROBOTS DO YOUR FIGHTING FOR YOU AMBASSADOR?!

CORRECT, CAPTAIN ADAMA.

WE DO.

NO, IT CAN'T BE! OUR AMBASSADOR IS...

...A ROBOT?!?

NOW MAY I HAVE THAT LASER PISTOL CAPTAIN?

Y-YES, YOUR EXCELLENCY!

HUMANS OF SCORPIA, HEAR ME.

TODAY THE CYLONS MEAN TO SWEEP OVER US--TOMORROW THEY WILL TRY TO SWEEP ASIDE OUR WAY OF LIFE.

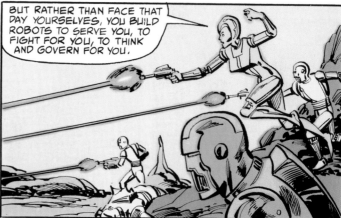

BUT RATHER THAN FACE THAT DAY YOURSELVES, YOU BUILD ROBOTS TO SERVE YOU, TO FIGHT FOR YOU, TO THINK AND GOVERN FOR YOU.

AND, BECAUSE WE CHERISH THE LIFE YOU GAVE US, WE WILL SERVE, AND FIGHT, AND THINK, AND GOVERN--

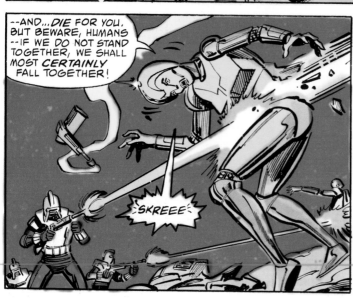

--AND... DIE FOR YOU. BUT BEWARE, HUMANS --IF WE DO NOT STAND TOGETHER, WE SHALL MOST CERTAINLY FALL TOGETHER!

SKREEE

GODS OF KOBOL!

NUMB WITH HORROR, COMMANDER ADAMA REMEMBERS HIS MIND GOING BLANK!

AND TO THIS DAY HE CANNOT EXPLAIN WHY HE DID WHAT HE DID NEXT!

DIRTY CYLON MURDERERS!

THE CAPRICANS ARE CRAZY--RISKING THEIR LIVES FOR A ROBOT!

B-BUT THE AMBASSADOR RISKED HER LIFE TO SAVE OURS!

THEY DON'T STAND A CHANCE! WHAT THEY'RE DOING IS SUICIDE!

"AND IF THEY FALL-- WHAT HAPPENS TO US?!"

TIGH, GET BACK TO COVER!

CAN'T HEAR YOU, ADAMA! MY EARS ARE LASER-SHOCKED!

VEEP

VIP

VIP

VREEP

GODS! LASER PISTOL'S JAMMED--AND THE CYLONS ARE CLOSING FAST! TIGH OLD FRIEND, THIS IS THE....

VREEP

...END?!?

VIP

VEEP

VIP

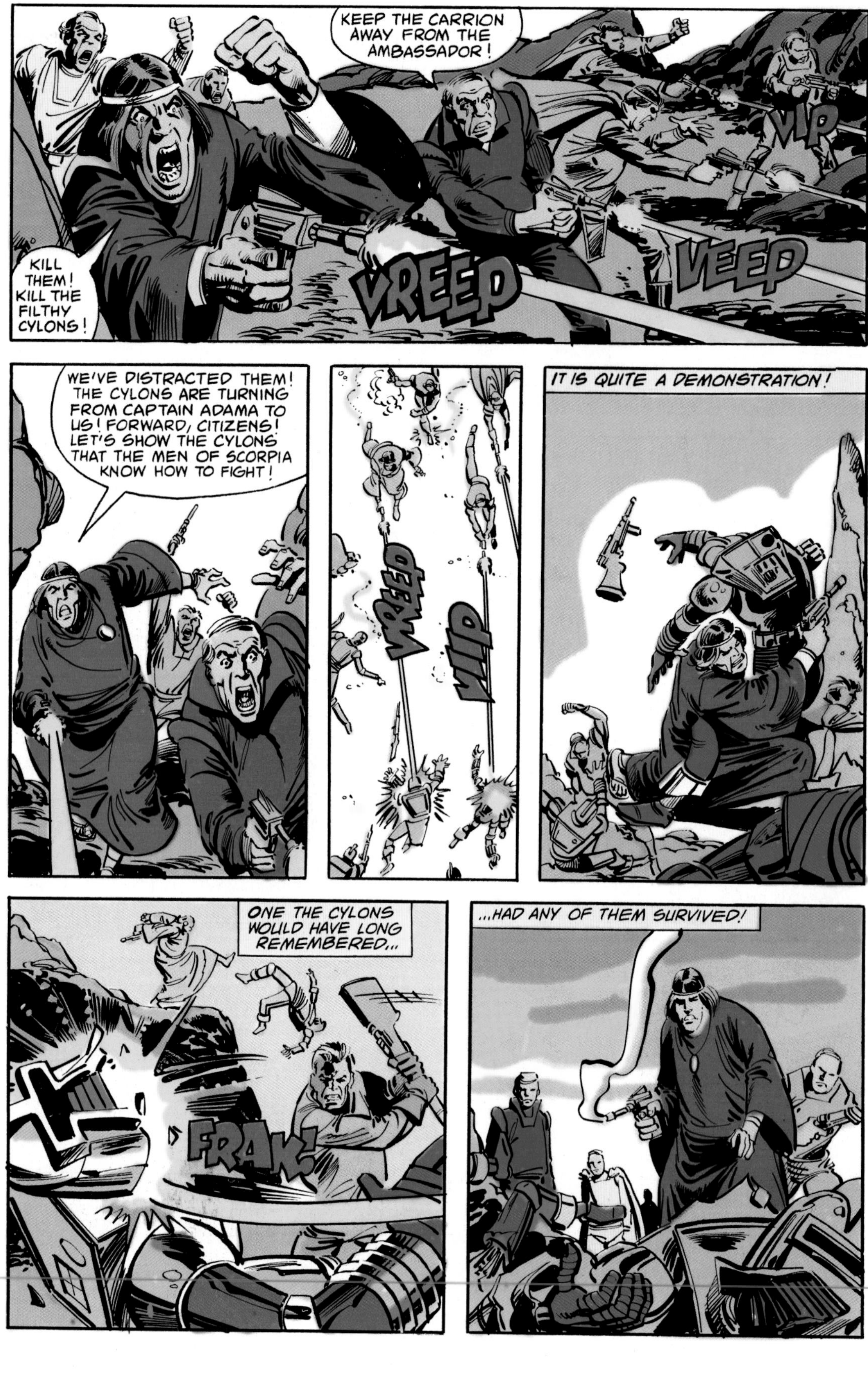
KEEP THE CARRION AWAY FROM THE AMBASSADOR!
VIP
KILL THEM! KILL THE FILTHY CYLONS!
VREEP
VEEP
WE'VE DISTRACTED THEM! THE CYLONS ARE TURNING FROM CAPTAIN ADAMA TO US! FORWARD, CITIZENS! LET'S SHOW THE CYLONS THAT THE MEN OF SCORPIA KNOW HOW TO FIGHT!
VREEP
VIIP
IT IS QUITE A DEMONSTRATION!
ONE THE CYLONS WOULD HAVE LONG REMEMBERED...
FRAK!
...HAD ANY OF THEM SURVIVED!

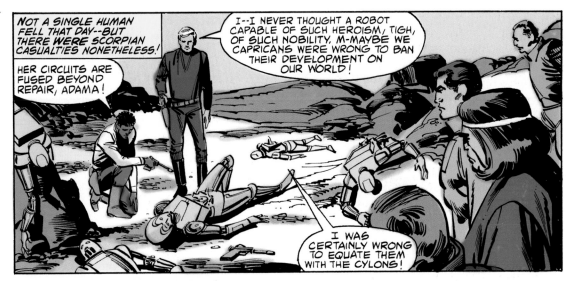

NEXT MONTH: **MUTINY!** ON SALE AUG. 7

There are those who believe life here began out there, far across the universe, with tribes of humans who may have been the forefathers of the Egyptians. Or the Toltecs. Or the Mayans. Some believe there may yet be brothers of man who even now fight to survive somewhere beyond the heavens!

STAN LEE PRESENTS: **BattlestaR GALACTICA** ™ •

Based on the television series Battlestar Galactica™ * written and created by Glen Larson.

# SPACE-MIMIC!

WITH CYLON RAIDERS DOGGING THEIR TRAIL, SIRE URI'S LUST FOR POWER THREATENS TO TEAR THE FRAGILE UNITY OF THE FLEET APART...FROM WITHIN!

YOUR PRIVATE GUARDS NEARLY KILLED MY FATHER, URI!

EASY, APOLLO! URI MAY BE A SLUG OF THE LOWEST ORDER, BUT HE'S STILL PRESIDENT OF THE COUNCIL OF TWELVE!

A POSITION HE *STOLE* FROM MY FATHER AFTER HE ENTERED THE MEMORY STIMULATOR, STARBUCK!

THE PLOT FAILED, ATHENA, AND YOUR FATHER--COMMANDER ADAMA--IS ALL RIGHT! BUT NOW THE FLEET FACES AN EVEN GREATER DANGER!

A-AND WE FACE IT... LEADERLESS!

**BILL MANTLO** • **SAL BUSCEMA & KLAUS JANSON** • WATANABE & COSTANZA • BOB SHAREN • **AL MILGROM** • **J. SHOOTER**
SCRIBE • NAVIGATORS • LETTERERS • COLORIST • OVERSEER • COMMANDER

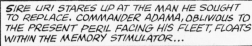

SIRE URI STARES UP AT THE MAN HE SOUGHT TO REPLACE. COMMANDER ADAMA, OBLIVIOUS TO THE PRESENT PERIL FACING HIS FLEET, FLOATS WITHIN THE MEMORY STIMULATOR...

...WHERE HE SEARCHES THE BY-WAYS OF HIS MEMORY FOR AN ARCHAIC INSCRIPTION HE GLANCED BRIEFLY ON THE PLANET KOBOL.

AN INSCRIPTION THAT POINTS THE WAY TO THE MYTHICAL PLANET, EARTH!

I-ISN'T THERE SOME WAY TO REACH ADAMA?

NOT WITHOUT ENDANGERING HIS SANITY, URI!

AND NOW, WITH THE CONTROLS DESTROYED, ADAMA MAY NEVER ESCAPE!

YOU WOULD HAVE DOOMED HIM TO RELIVE HIS PAST FOR ALL ETERNITY JUST SO YOU COULD SEIZE THE PRESIDENCY OF THE COUNCIL OF TWELVE, URI!

EASY, APOLLO!

SORRY, COLONEL TIGH, BUT I FIND IT AWFULLY HARD TO RESTRAIN MY TEMPER IN THE PRESENCE OF THIS...THIS TRAITOR! HE DID EVERYTHING HE COULD TO UNDERMINE MY FATHER'S COMMAND, INCLUDING HIJACKING SHIPS OF THE FLEET TO MAKE IT LOOK LIKE ADAMA WAS INCAPABLE OF LEADERSHIP.

"THEN HE TRIED TO HAVE MY FATHER ASSASSINATED WHILE HE FLOATED HELPLESSLY WITHIN THE MEMORY STIMULATOR.

"ONLY BECAUSE I DISOBEYED ORDERS TO GO ON A SCOUTING MISSION, AND STAYED ON BOARD THE GALACTICA, WAS I ABLE TO SAVE MY FATHER'S LIFE."

YOU WRONG ME, CAPTAIN APOLLO! I ADMIT MY MEN WERE SOMEWHAT OVER-ZEALOUS IN TRANS-LATING MY DENUNCIATIONS OF COMMANDER ADAMA INTO POLITICAL ASSAS-SINATION--

--BUT, YOU FORGET, IT WAS *I* WHO WARNED YOU IN TIME TO STOP THEM!

YOU LYING SLUG! YOU ONLY PANICKED AFTER IT TURNED OUT THE FLEET'S FOOD SUPPLY *AGRO-SHIP* REALLY *WAS* MISSING --AND NOT HIJACKED BY YOUR MEN!

CREATING ONE FRACK OF A MESS THAT YOU DIDN'T HAVE THE GUTS TO DEAL WITH!

WITHOUT THE AGRO-SHIP WE WON'T BE ABLE TO FEED THE FLEET, COLONEL TIGH.

I KNOW, CAPTAIN. IT'S A SITUATION THAT DEMANDS OUR IMMEDIATE ATTENTION.

SIRE URI IS NOMINAL PRESIDENT OF THE COUNCIL, AND WE CAN'T JUDGE HIM UNTIL THE COUNCIL RECONVENES. MEANWHILE, HE AND HIS AD-HERENTS WILL BE PLACED UNDER HOUSE ARREST!

WHO DO WE REPORT TO THEN, COLONEL TIGH?

TO ME, BOOMER. AS SECOND-IN-COMMAND TO COMMANDER ADAMA, I'M TAKING CHARGE OF THE GALACTICA AND THE FLEET!

HMMPH! SIRE URI SEEMS TO HAVE GOT-TEN OFF LIGHTLY, DOCTOR WILKER!

COLONEL TIGH IS IN AN AWKWARD SIT-UATION, CASSIOPEA. HE KNOWS HE CAN'T CONDEMN A MAN OF URI'S POSITION--BUT HE'S ALSO GOT TO THINK OF THE SAFETY OF THE FLEET.

THE DESTRUCTION OF THE TWELVE PLANETS HAS FORCED US ALL TO MAKE PAINFUL DECISIONS.

PERHAPS EVEN URI THOUGHT HIS WAY WAS THE RIGHT ONE.

YOU'RE TOO FORGIVING, DOCTOR.

I KNOW, CASSIOPEA. THAT'S WHY I'M A PHYSICIAN...

...AND NOT A WARRIOR!

FELGERCARB! IT'S A GOOD THING ATHENA, BOOMER AND I RETURNED TO THE GALACTICA IN TIME OR URI MIGHT HAVE TRIED A FULL-SCALE COUP!

BUT WHAT COULD HAVE HAPPENED TO THE AGRO-SHIP? IT COULDN'T JUST UP AND VANISH!

THAT'S SOMETHING WE'D BETTER ANSWER, AND FAST, ATHENA! MEANWHILE, I'M ORDERING STRICT RATIONING THROUGHOUT THE FLEET!

I DON'T KNOW. WITH THE AGRO-SHIP MISSING, URI'S SCARED. HE KNOWS HE CAN'T LEAD WITH A FAMINE FACING THE FLEET!

RATIONING? THAT WILL IMMEDIATELY TIP OFF THE FACT THAT SOMETHING'S WRONG!

AREN'T YOU AFRAID OF PANICKING OUR PEOPLE, COLONEL?

WHAT OTHER CHOICE DO WE HAVE, APOLLO? UNLESS WE CUT BACK ON CONSUMPTION--

--THE FLEET WILL RUN OUT OF FOOD IN LESS THAN A WEEK! I'D RATHER DEAL WITH A PANIC NOW THAN SLOW STARVATION LATER!

SO THE QUESTION REMAINS: WHAT HAPPENED TO THE AGRO-SHIP? THE GALACTICA WOULD SEEM TO BE A SUITABLE GUARDIAN FOR ITS DEPENDENT FLOCK OF SMALLER SHIPS.

YET, IN ATTEPTING TO OUTRACE THE PURSUING CYLONS, IS IT POSSIBLE THAT THE GALACTICA HAS LEFT SOME OF THE SUB-LIGHT SPEED SHIPS BEHIND?

IT'S THAT VERY POSSIBILITY THAT HAS HAD MASTER-TECH SHADRACK WORKING OVERTIME TO CONVERT THE ENTIRE FLEET TO LIGHT-SPEED DRIVE, BEFORE THE CYLONS CAN AGAIN LOCATE THEIR PREY!

RESEAL ALL AERO-SLEEVES ON THAT CRUISER, JUNIOR-TECH WHITTAKER.

I'M TENDING TO IT RIGHT NOW, MASTER-TECH SHADRACK.

BUT, AS JUNIOR-TECH WHITTAKER IGNITES HIS LASER-WELDER...

EH? THAT STRANGE SILVER GLOW--?!

IT SEEMS TO BE BECKONING TO ME!

I-I CAN'T RESIST REACHING OUT TO IT--!

BY THE GODS! IT-IT'S LIKE FIRE, BURNING THROUGH ME!

M-MOVING ALONG MY HAND-- MY ARM! D-DOING SOMETHING TO MY...

...MIND. JUNIOR-TECH WHITTAKER CEASES TO FEEL ANY PAIN...

...AND THE STRANGE SILVER GLOW BEGINS TO SHIFT FROM SHAPELESSNESS, MOMENTARILY GIVING WAY TO AN ALIEN, INHUMAN FORM--THEN SHIMMERING AGAIN AS THE ALIEN, CLUTCHING WHITTAKER'S HAND, *BECOMES* A MIRROR IMAGE OF THE SENSELESS JUNIOR-TECH HIMSELF!

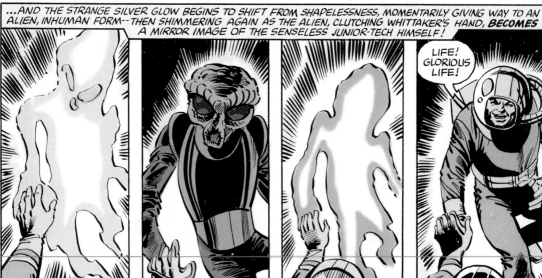

LIFE! GLORIOUS LIFE!

FOR COUNTLESS EONS I HAVE FLOATED IN THIS COLD AND LIFE-LESS VOID, WAITING FOR CONTACT WITH ANOTHER LIVING, BREATHING FORM TO FREE ME--

--FROM THE *STASIS SPHERE* IN WHICH I WAS IMPRISONED.

THIS ENTITY HAS GIVEN ME LIFE AGAIN.

A PITY IT WAS AT THE COST OF HIS OWN.

*WITHOUT THE SLIGHTEST TRACE OF REMORSE, THE ALIEN IMPOSTER SEVERS JUNIOR-TECH WHITTAKER'S LIFELINE...*

*...THEN, AS THE DYING SPACEMAN FLOATS OFF INTO THE VOID, THE CREATURE DIRECTS ITS MALEVOLENT ATTENTIONS TOWARD MASTER-TECH SHADRACK!*

FINISHED RESEALING THOSE AEROSLEEVES ALREADY, WHITTAKER!

YES, MASTER-TECH!

AND NOW THIS PRIMITIVE WELDING TOOL WILL MAKE AN END OF *YOU!*

*MASTER-TECH SHADRACK SEEMS OBLIVIOUS TO HIS FATE...*

*... WHILE APOLLO, ATHENA AND STARBUCK MEET WITH CHIEF-OF-SHIP'S STORES **EDIK** IN THE GALACTICA'S COMMISSARY.*

WHAT YOU SEE BE-FORE YOU ARE THE FLEET'S FOOD STORES, MY FRIENDS. MOST ARE SUPPLIED BY THE AGRO-SHIP'S HYDROPONIC TANKS.

HOW LONG WOULD THE PRESENT SUPPLY LAST, CHIEF EDIK?

OH, MY, NO MORE THAN A WEEK!

OUR STORAGE SPACE IS QUITE LIMITED!

HOW LONG COULD WE LAST WITH RATIONING, CHIEF EDIK?

YOU MEAN WITH **STRICT** RATIONING?

≥ULP!≤

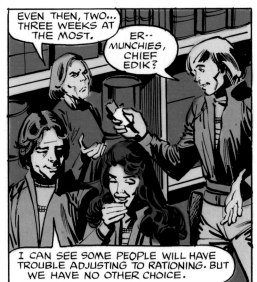

EVEN THEN, TWO... THREE WEEKS AT THE MOST.

ER-- MUNCHIES, CHIEF EDIK?

I CAN SEE SOME PEOPLE WILL HAVE TROUBLE ADJUSTING TO RATIONING. BUT WE HAVE NO OTHER CHOICE.

AW, I'VE GOT WHAT IT TAKES, CAPTAIN.

I JUST WANTED TO GIVE MY SWEET-TOOTH ONE FINAL TASTE OF WHAT IT WOULD BE MISSING.

OOH! MUNCHIES! CAN MUFFEY AND ME HAVE A CANDY BAR, UNCLE STARBUCK?

MUNCHIES? WHAT MUNCHIES?

THE ONES BEHIND YOUR BACK, UNCLE STARBUCK!

YIPE

STARBUCK, YOU SHOULD BE ASHAMED OF YOURSELF, HOARDING YOUR WEEKLY RATION AWAY FROM A BOY AND HIS DAGGIT.

UH...RIGHT! I MEANT TO SHARE IT, CAPTAIN!

WHINE

THERE'S ONE FOR EACH OF US, MUFFEY! BEG, BOY!

BUT THE GENERAL LAUGHTER SUBSIDES AS THE HISSING OF A NEARBY AIRLOCK REMINDS THE CREW OF THE GALACTICA THAT EVERY MOMENT THEY SPEND IN THE VOID SPELLS ...DANGER!

APOLLO! STARBUCK! **LOOK!!**

AYE, TAKE A GOOD LOOK, ATHENA, AND THEN EXPLAIN WHY A JUNIOR OFFICER WOULD TRY TO **MURDER** HIS SUPERIOR?

DESPITE HIS GRIM DEMEANOR, IT IS IMMEDIATELY EVIDENT FROM HIS ASHEN FEATURES THAT MASTER-TECH SHADRACK IS...**SCARED!**

WHAT HAPPENED, MASTER-TECH?

WE WERE CONVERTING THE SHIPS OF THE FLEET TO LIGHT-DRIVE...

"...WHEN WHITTAKER CAME AT ME WITH HIS LASER-TORCH!"

"I CLIPPED HIM--"

"--AND HE FOLDED LIKE A MARIONETTE WHOSE STRINGS'VE BEEN CUT!"

SOON, IN THE GALACTICA'S SICK BAY...

ANY DIAGNOSIS YET, DR. SPANG?

A VERY SIMPLE ONE, CAPTAIN APOLLO. THIS MAN IS...DEAD!

WHAT?!

I-I DIDN'T THINK I HIT HIM HARD ENOUGH TO... TO KILL HIM!

YOU STRUCK IN SELF-DEFENSE, MASTER-TECH SHADRACK!

EXCUSE ME A MOMENT, ATHENA. I SAID THIS MAN IS DEAD--

--BUT IT WASN'T A BLOW FROM A MECHANIC'S WRENCH THAT KILLED HIM!

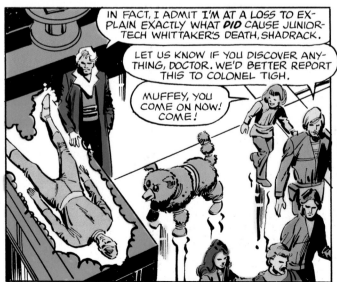

IN FACT, I ADMIT I'M AT A LOSS TO EXPLAIN EXACTLY WHAT DID CAUSE JUNIOR-TECH WHITTAKER'S DEATH, SHADRACK.

LET US KNOW IF YOU DISCOVER ANYTHING, DOCTOR. WE'D BETTER REPORT THIS TO COLONEL TIGH.

MUFFEY, YOU COME ON NOW! COME!

THE OTHERS DEPART, LEAVING A PUZZLED DR. SPANG ALONE WITH THE CORPSE.

I DIDN'T KNOW HOW TO TELL APOLLO, BUT SOMETHING'S TERRIBLY WRONG!

MY INSTRUMENTS REVEAL THAT JUNIOR-TECH WHITTAKER WAS NEVER ALIVE!

BUT THAT'S IMPOSSIBLE! I HAVE PRINTOUTS, MED-EXAMS OF WHITTAKER! THERE WAS ABSOLUTELY NOTHING UNUSUAL ABOUT HIM! THAT LEAVES BUT ONE CONCLUSION...

THE CORPSE ON MY EXAMINING COUCH IS *NOT* JUNIOR-TECH WHITTAKER--

--BUT SOMETHING COMPLETELY...

EH? WHAT IN--?!

ARRGHH!!

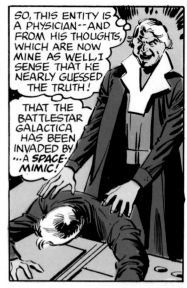

SO, THIS ENTITY IS A PHYSICIAN--AND FROM HIS THOUGHTS, WHICH ARE NOW MINE AS WELL, I SENSE THAT HE NEARLY GUESSED THE TRUTH!

THAT THE BATTLESTAR GALACTICA HAS BEEN INVADED BY ...A *SPACE-MIMIC!*

I CAN TAKE NO CHANCES ON SPANG WAKING TO REVEAL MY DECEPTION!

THIS PNEUMO-NEEDLE WILL INJECT DRUGS INTO HIS BLOODSTREAM WHICH WILL KILL THE GOOD DOCTOR INSTANTANEOUSLY!

LEAVING ONLY MYSELF AS THE SUBSTITUTE SPANG.

WHILE, IN THE CORRIDOR OUTSIDE...

BOXEY, WHAT'S WRONG WITH MUFFEY?

SKRATCH WHINE SKRATCH

I DON'T KNOW, AUNTY 'THENA! THAT DEAD MAN MADE HIM ACT REAL FUNNY!

DEAD MAN? HMM. MAYBE WE SHOULD ASK THE DOCTOR IF HE CAN EXPLAIN...

...WHY A CORPSE WOULD BOTHER A ROBOT DAGGIT!

GREAT PLANETS!

DR. SPANG'S ABOUT TO BE MURDERED BY...BY DR. SPANG?!?

THE DOPPEL-GANGER DOCTOR SNARLS...

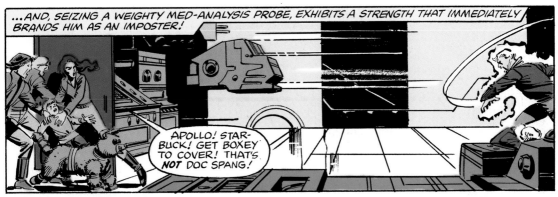

...AND, SEIZING A WEIGHTY MED-ANALYSIS PROBE, EXHIBITS A STRENGTH THAT IMMEDIATELY BRANDS HIM AS AN IMPOSTER!

APOLLO! STARBUCK! GET BOXEY TO COVER! THAT'S **NOT** DOC SPANG!

SHRAK! SHRAK

WE FIGURED THAT OUT FOR OURSELVES, ATHENA!

SO WHO --OR WHAT --IS HE?!

THE SPACE-MIMIC PROVIDES NO ANSWER AS IT ABANDONS ITS ATTEMPT TO SLAY THE REAL DOCTOR...

...AND FLEES THROUGH A FAR DOOR INTO THE GALACTICA'S MYRIAD CORRIDORS!

WE CAN'T LET THAT GUY GET AWAY!

WE'VE GOT TO CHECK OUT THE DOCTOR FIRST! HE'S WAKING UP!

COLD! SO COLD!

CAPTAIN, THE DAGGIT'S GOT OUR IMPOSTER'S SCENT!

YIPE YIPE

DON'T ANYONE EVER TELL ME THAT ROBOT ISN'T AS GOOD AS A REAL DAGGIT!

WE WON'T! LEAVE BOXEY WITH DOC SPANG. GO ON, MUFFEY, LEAD US TO OUR UNINVITED VISITOR!

YIPE YARF

AT THAT MOMENT, OUTSIDE THE GALACTICA'S INTERROGATION ROOM HOUSING THE MEMORY MACHINE...

DOC SPANG! I THOUGHT YOU WERE IN THE INFIRMARY!

A NEW ENTITY! HOW MANY ARE ARE THERE ABOARD THIS VESSEL?

HOW MANY NEW LIFE-EXPERIENCES FOR ME TO ASSIMULATE?

YOU FEELING OKAY, DOC? YOU DON'T LOOK QUITE··

--YOURSELF!

THERE IS NO TIME FOR BOOMER TO EVEN SCREAM...

...AS THE SPACE MIMIC TAKES ON HIS APPEARANCE AND MEMORIES!

SO NOW I AM A FIGHTER-PILOT NAMED BOOMER, ASSIGNED TO STAND GUARD OVER THE BEING WHO COMMANDS THE GALACTICA!

"THAT IS THE BEING I MUST BECOME, IF I AM TO BE FREE TO PROWL THIS SHIP UNQUESTIONED, AN INSATIABLE PSYCHIC VAMPIRE!"

HMM. I THOUGHT I HEARD SOMETHING STRANGE? BUT THE MONITORS INDICATE THAT THE MEMORY STIMULATOR IS FUNCTIONING CORRECTLY...

...AND YOU'RE CERTAINLY ALRIGHT, AREN'T YOU, BOOMER?

YES, NURSE CASSIOPEA.

I'M FEELING JUST FINE!

IN THE CORRIDOR...

YIP YIP

LOOK! IT'S BOOMER!

BUT IS HE ALIVE, OR...?

HE'S ALIVE, PRAISE THE GODS, AND REGAINING CONSCIOUSNESS! BUT HE WAS STANDING GUARD OVER...

COMMANDER ADAMA!!

COME ON, STARBUCK! THERE'S NOT A MOMENT TO LOSE!

YIPE

COLD! MY BLOOD FEELS LIKE ICE!

APPREHENSIVE OVER THE FATE OF COMMANDER ADAMA WHO FLOATS HELPLESSLY WITHIN THE MEMORY MACHINE, APOLLO AND STARBUCK CHARGE INTO THE PRESENCE OF...

NURSE CASSIOPEA?

TWO NURSE CASSIOPEAS, STARBUCK-- BUT WHICH IS THE REAL ONE?!

C-CAPTAIN APOLLO, THANK HEAVEN YOU'RE HERE! I-I WAS TENDING TO YOUR FATHER WHEN I SENSED SOMEONE BEHIND ME!

WHINE

I-IT LOOKED LIKE BOOMER-- BUT AS SOON AS IT TOUCHED ME, I-IT BECAME-- ME!

D-DON'T YOU BELIEVE ME? WHAT ARE YOU STARING AT?

THE DAGGIT!

MUFFEY--

WHY, THE DAGGIT PROBABLY SENSES THAT MY DOUBLE IS AN ALIEN. SURELY YOU DON'T HAVE ANY DOUBTS THAT I'M THE REAL CASSIOPEA...?

YIP YIP

WHINE

BUT MUFFEY WAS CREATED WITH ALL THE SENSES OF A REAL DAGGIT...

...AND THE LITTLE ROBOT IS ABLE TO DISTINGU-ISH BETWEEN THE SCENT OF FINE, GENTLE CASSIOPEA-- AND THE SCENT OF AN ALIEN!

ARF! ARF!

NO! KEEP AWAY FROM ME, YOU MECHANICAL MOCKERY!

YIIIPE

YOU ARE NOT EVEN ALIVE YOURSELF--

--HOW COULD YOU ROB *ME* OF MY CHANCE AT LIFE?!

I GUESS WE KNOW WHICH CASSIOPEA'S A PHONY, RIGHT, CAPTAIN?

LET'S HOPE WE LIVE LONG ENOUGH TO USE THAT INFORMATION, LIEUTENANT!

THAT YOU WILL NOT DO, HUMANS, FOR I NEED ONLY DISPOSE OF YOU TWO AND THE UNCONSCIOUS NURSE--

ZRAK

--AND MY PRESENCE ABOARD THE GALACTICA WILL NEVER BE REVEALED!

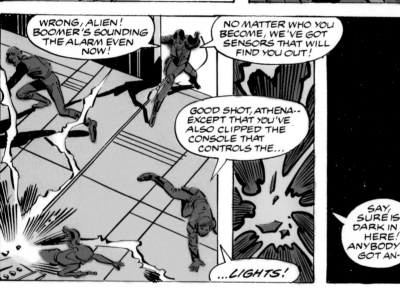

WRONG, ALIEN! BOOMER'S SOUNDING THE ALARM EVEN NOW!

NO MATTER WHO YOU BECOME, WE'VE GOT SENSORS THAT WILL FIND YOU OUT!

GOOD SHOT, ATHENA-- EXCEPT THAT YOU'VE ALSO CLIPPED THE CONSOLE THAT CONTROLS THE...

...LIGHTS!

--IGNITER? OH, YEAH, I DO!

SAY, SURE IS DARK IN HERE! ANYBODY GOT AN--

SKRIT

THERE! THE SPACE MIMIC?

UNH-UH, ATHENA! DON'T ASK ME HOW I KNOW, BUT SOMETHING TELLS ME THAT'S OUR *REAL* NURSE CASSIOPEA!

OH! W-WHAT HAPPENED? W-WHY DO I FEEL SO *COLD*?!

SHE'S EXHIBITING THE SAME SYMPTOMS AS BOOMER AND DOC SPANG WHEN THEY CAME TO! BUT IF SHE'S THE REAL CASSIOPEA, THEN WHERE...?

CAPTAIN APOLLO, I DEMAND AN EXPLANA- TION! HOW COULD COMMANDER ADAMA LEAVE THE MEMORY MACHINE WITHOUT NEWS OF IT BEING REPORTED TO THE...

...C-COUNCIL ?!?

I-I DON'T UNDERSTAND! IF YOUR FATHER IS STILL INSIDE THE MEMORY STIMULATOR, THEN WHO WAS THAT COMMANDER ADAMA THAT JUST PASSED ME ON HIS WAY TO THE BRIDGE ?!?

THE *SPACE-MIMIC!*

IT MUST HAVE TAKEN ON YOUR FATHER'S IDENTITY THROUGH CONTACT WITH THE MEMORY MACHINE'S CIRCUITRY!

AND IF IT REACHES THE BRIDGE, IT WILL TAKE COMMAND OF THE GALACTICA!

LET'S GO!!

WAIT! I DEMAND TO KNOW WHAT'S GOING ON!!

VIPE VIPE

BOOMER! DID YOU SEE ANY SIGN OF THE ALIEN?

NOT ME, CAPTAIN! THE ONLY ONE TO GO BY HERE WAS COMMANDER ADAMA--

--AND HE TOLD ME TO SWITCH THE SENSORS OFF!

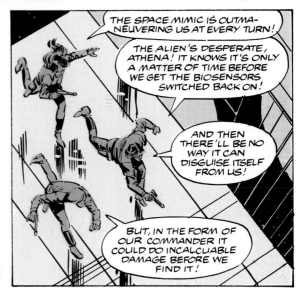

THE SPACE MIMIC IS OUTMANEUVERING US AT EVERY TURN!

THE ALIEN'S DESPERATE, ATHENA! IT KNOWS IT'S ONLY A MATTER OF TIME BEFORE WE GET THE BIOSENSORS SWITCHED BACK ON!

AND THEN THERE'LL BE NO WAY IT CAN DISGUISE ITSELF FROM US!

BUT, IN THE FORM OF OUR COMMANDER IT COULD DO INCALCUABLE DAMAGE BEFORE WE FIND IT!

APOLLO NODS GRIMLY IN RESPONSE TO STARBUCK'S STATEMENT, WHILE, IN THE CORRIDORS AHEAD...

...THE COUNTERFEIT COMMANDER ADAMA PRESSES ON IN HOPES OF ELUDING HIS PURSUERS!

THIS ENTITY'S MEMORIES ARE SO STRONG--

--ALMOST OVERWHELMING ME WITH CONCERN FOR THE FRAIL HUMANS ABOARD THIS VESSEL! HE CARES FOR--*LOVES*--ALL OF THEM!

LOOK, SETH! IT'S COMMANDER ADAMA!

GREETINGS, COMMANDER! MY WIFE AND I HAVE NOT HAD A CHANCE TO THANK YOU SINCE THE CYLON TREACHERY AT THE SIGNING OF THE PEACE TREATY. ONLY YOUR PRESENCE OF MIND SAVED US FROM DYING WITH CAPRICA, OUR WORLD!

AND EVERYWHERE THE ASTONISHED ALIEN GOES WITHIN THE GREAT BATTLESTAR GALACTICA, THE STORY IS THE SAME!

FOR ALL THE PERIL OF THEIR PRESENT PLIGHT, THERE IS HARDLY A MAN, WOMAN OR CHILD ABOARD WHO DOES NOT OWE SOME DEBT OF THANKS TO COMMANDER ADAMA.

AND, IN EXPRESSING THEIR GRATITUDE, THESE SURVIVORS OF HUMANITY RENDER FREELY TO THE SPACE-MIMIC EMOTIONS HE WOULD OTHERWISE HAVE SOUGHT TO *STEAL!*

AND THIS MASSIVE INPOURING OF AFFECTION BEGINS TO HAVE ITS EFFECT UPON THE ALIEN!

T-THEY LOVE THIS COMMANDER ADAMA! THEY HOLD NOTHING BACK FROM HIM!

IT IS TOO MUCH TO ABSORB--! TOO MUCH!

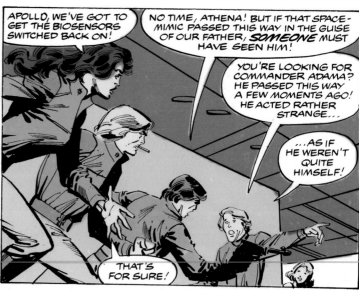

APOLLO, WE'VE GOT TO GET THE BIOSENSORS SWITCHED BACK ON!

NO TIME, ATHENA! BUT IF THAT SPACE-MIMIC PASSED THIS WAY IN THE GUISE OF OUR FATHER, *SOMEONE* MUST HAVE SEEN HIM!

YOU'RE LOOKING FOR COMMANDER ADAMA? HE PASSED THIS WAY A FEW MOMENTS AGO! HE ACTED RATHER STRANGE...

...AS IF HE WEREN'T QUITE HIMSELF!

THAT'S FOR SURE!

AND THIS CORRIDOR LEADS DIRECTLY TO THE BRIDGE, OUR ALIEN FRIEND OBVIOUSLY INTENDS TO TAKE CONTROL OF...

THERE HE GOES!

ALL RIGHT, CREATURE! YOU'VE HAD YOUR LITTLE JAUNT IN OTHER PEOPLE'S BODIES! COME AWAY FROM THE CONTROL CONSOLE AND GIVE YOURSELF UP!

NO! I MUST NOT BE RETURNED TO NON-LIFE!

YOU WON'T MAKE ME GIVE UP WITHOUT A...

...FIGHT, APOLLO?

SON?

GODS OF KOBOL, THE CREATURE THINKS IT REALLY *IS* FATHER!

B-BUT I AM ADAMA! YOU KNOW ME, DON'T YOU...

...ATHENA?

IT'S THE MEMORY STIMULATOR! FATHER WAS IN IT WHEN THE SPACE-MIMIC DUPLICATED HIM!

MAKING THE STOLEN MEMORIES SO INTENSE THAT THEY SEEM REAL!

PLEASE, PLEASE SAY YOU UNDERSTAND! I LOVE YOU SON --DAUGHTER! I-I WOULDN'T HURT YOU...

...STARBUCK,

OH, *FRACK!*

YOU LOVE ME! HATE ME! LOVE ME! HATE ME!

I AM ADAMA! NOT ADAMA!

LOOKS LIKE AN OVERLOAD, IF YOU ASK ME!

THE ALIEN CAN'T STAND THE EMOTIONS FLOODING OVER IT! THEY'RE TOO...

...HUMAN!

MUST KILL TO SURVIVE! MUST SLAY ADAMA'S CHILDREN!

BUT... THIS ENTITY... IS ADAMA! INFANTI- CIDE! CANNOT... SLAY MY OWN... CHILDREN!

NOT MINE! NOT MINE! NOT ADAMA! BUT IF NOT...

...THEN WHO/ WHAT/ WHY/ AM I?

NO LIFE THAT IS NOT STOLEN FROM OTHERS! NO LIFE...

...NO LIIIIFE!!

FELGERCARB! I-I THINK I'M GOING TO BE SICK!

THE CREATURE HAD TO ABSORB THE LIFE- ESSENCES OF OTHERS IN ORDER TO SURVIVE! WITHOUT DOING SO, IT HAD NO FORM, NO LIFE!

BUT, IN *BECOMING* MY FATHER --COMMANDER ADAMA-- IT ALSO BECAME POSSESSED OF AN OVERWHELMING SENSE OF MORALITY...OF AN INABILITY TO DO EVIL!

AND SO STRONG DID THAT MORAL RESPONSIBILITY BECOME, THAT IT CHOSE TO DESTROY ITSELF--

--RATHER THAN DESTROY THREE BEINGS FOR WHOM ITS HOST-BODY HELDAN OVER- WHELMING... LOVE!

NEXT **THIS PLANET HUNGERS...** ON SALE IN SEPT.

# #10

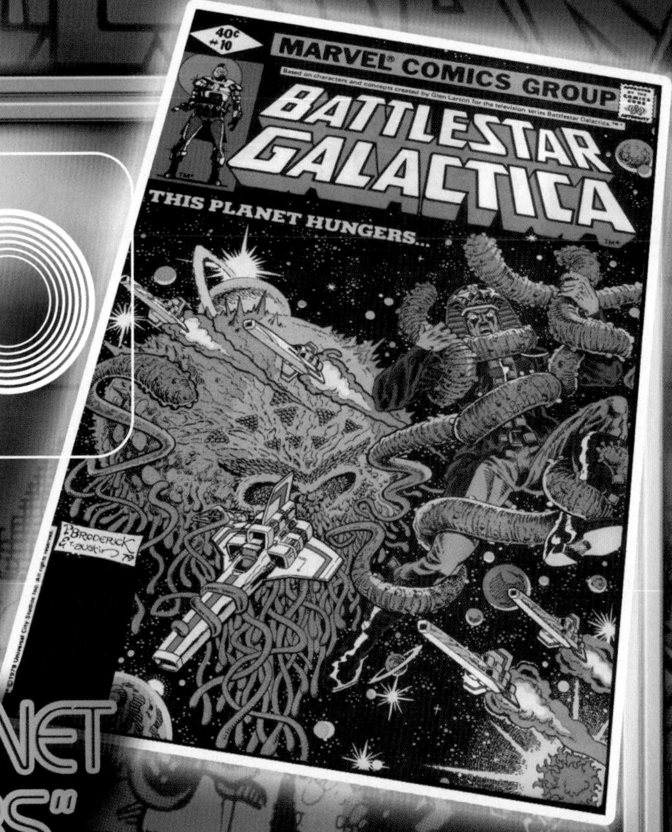
40¢ #10
MARVEL COMICS GROUP
BATTLESTAR GALACTICA
THIS PLANET HUNGERS...

## "THIS PLANET HUNGERS"

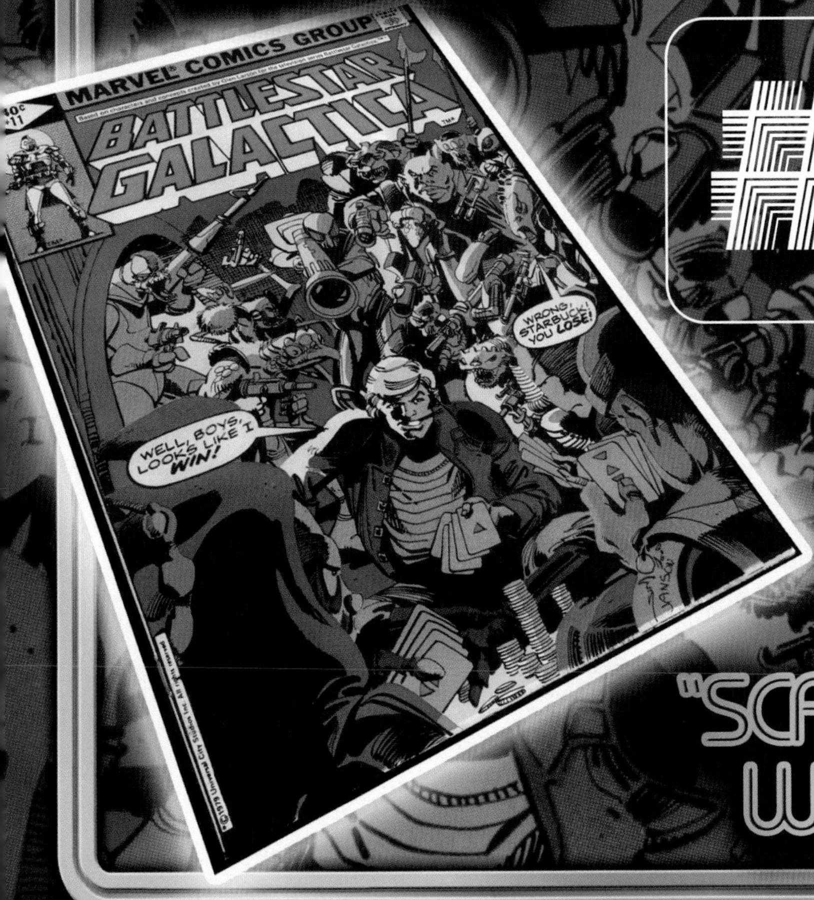
MARVEL COMICS GROUP
BATTLESTAR GALACTICA
WRONG, STARBUCK! YOU LOSE!
WELL, BOYS, LOOKS LIKE I WIN!

# #11

## "SCAVENGE WORLD"

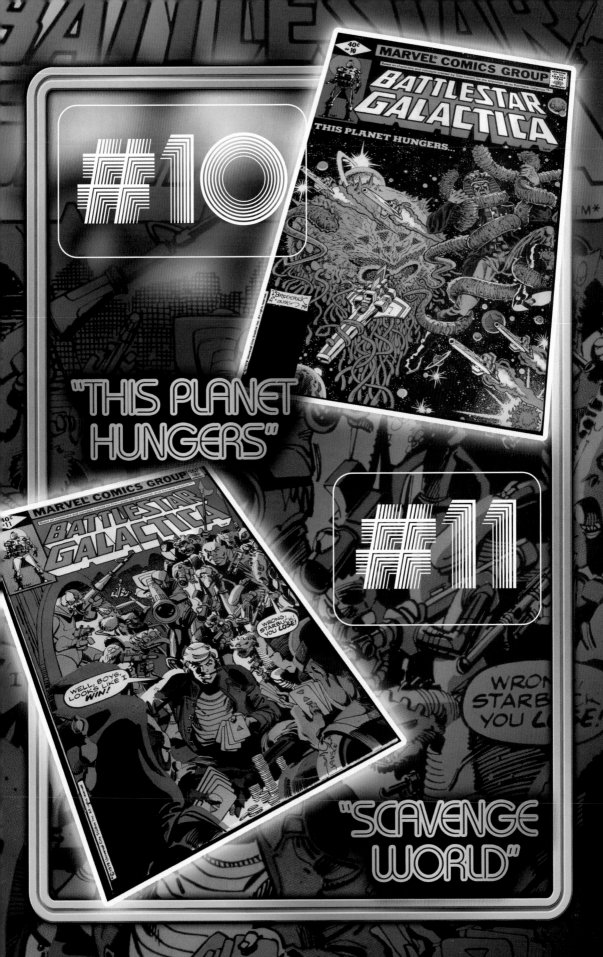

There are those who believe life here began out there, far across the universe, with tribes of humans who may have been the forefathers of the Egyptians. Or the Toltecs. Or the Mayans. Some believe there may yet be brothers of man who even now fight to survive somewhere beyond the heavens!

# STAN LEE PRESENTS: BattlestaR GALACTICA™

Based on the television series Battlestar Galactica™ written and created by Glen Larson.

TOM DEFALCO
words
•
PAT BRODERICK
pencils
•
BARRETO & MARCOS
inks
•
JOHN COSTANZA
letters
•
BEN SEAN
colors
•
ALLEN MILGROM
editing
•
JIM SHOOTER
paychecks

LUCK-- WITHOUT IT, NOTHING CAN ENDURE THE HUNGRY MAW OF DEEP SPACE-- OR A COSMIC VOID-- FOR LONG!

WITH DARING, SKILL, KNOWLEDGE AND TECHNOLOGY, ANYONE CAN ATTEMPT A CROSSING OF THE ASTRAL OCEANS. BUT, WITHOUT A FRIENDLY SMILE FROM DAME FORTUNE, ONE CANNOT SURVIVE.

LEADING STARBUCK AND ATHENA BACK TO GALACTICA AFTER A BRIEF SCOUTING MISSION, CAPTAIN APOLLO IS TROUBLED BY A GRIM REALIZATION...

THE FLEET'S IN DANGER--

--AND WE MAY HAVE ALREADY EXHAUSTED OUR LAST RESERVE OF LUCK!

LF575

# THIS PLANET HUNGERS

STREAKING INTO THE LANDING BAY, THE THREE VIPERS ARE AUTOMATICALLY CLEANSED AND DECONTAMINATED BY SONIC WAVES...

BY ENTERING A STARLESS, TRACKLESS VOID, WE MANAGED TO TEMPORARILY ELUDE THE CYLONS--

--BUT WHILE WE'VE BEEN LAID UP HERE, CONVERTING OUR SLOWER CRAFT TO LIGHT-SPEED, SHIPS HAVE BEEN MYSTERIOUSLY VANISHING FROM THE FLEET!

THEN, THERE'S MY FATHER...

APOLLO'S THOUGHTS ARE CUT SHORT AS HE JOCKEYS HIS SLEEK FIGHTER INTO ITS LANDING BERTH. HIS ENGINE HAS BARELY CEASED HUMMING WHEN...

WHAT'S THE RUSH, APOLLO?

I'VE GOT TO GET TO THE INTERROGATION CHAMBER TO CHECK ON MY FATHER'S CONDITION!

BIG BROTHER, HAVE YOU FORGOTTEN THAT COMMANDER ADAMA IS ALSO MY FATHER? I'M COMING ALONG!

SHORTLY...

I'M SORRY BUT MASTER-TECH SHADRACK HAS BEEN UNABLE TO REPAIR THE DAMAGE TO THE COMPUTER CONTROL CONSOLE.

COLONEL TIGH, HAS THERE BEEN ANY CHANGE?

THEN, MY FATHER IS STILL HOPELESSLY TRAPPED IN THE MEMORY MACHINE?

YES.

ANY ATTEMPT TO REMOVE COMMANDER ADAMA FROM THE MEMORY STIMULATOR-- WILL RESULT IN PERMANENT DAMAGE TO HIS MIND!

WHY DID FATHER HAVE TO ENTER THAT TERRIBLE MACHINE? WHY?

YOU KNOW THE REASONS, ATHENA! WHAT CHOICE DID HE HAVE? WHAT CHOICE DID ANY OF US HAVE...

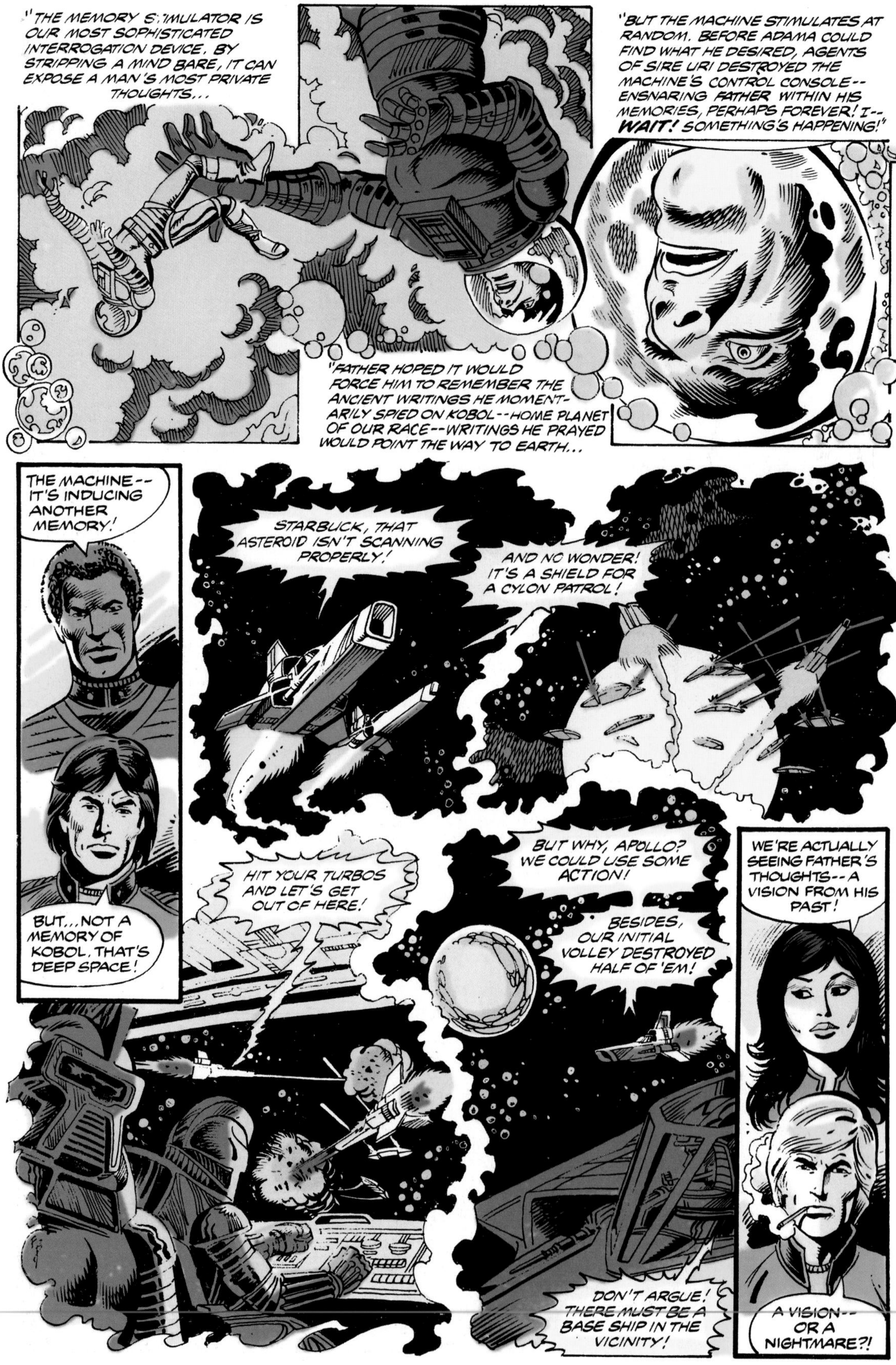
"THE MEMORY STIMULATOR IS OUR MOST SOPHISTICATED INTERROGATION DEVICE. BY STRIPPING A MIND BARE, IT CAN EXPOSE A MAN'S MOST PRIVATE THOUGHTS...
"FATHER HOPED IT WOULD FORCE HIM TO REMEMBER THE ANCIENT WRITINGS HE MOMENTARILY SPIED ON KOBOL--HOME PLANET OF OUR RACE--WRITINGS HE PRAYED WOULD POINT THE WAY TO EARTH...
"BUT THE MACHINE STIMULATES AT RANDOM. BEFORE ADAMA COULD FIND WHAT HE DESIRED, AGENTS OF SIRE URI DESTROYED THE MACHINE'S CONTROL CONSOLE--ENSNARING FATHER WITHIN HIS MEMORIES, PERHAPS FOREVER! I--WAIT! SOMETHING'S HAPPENING!"
THE MACHINE--IT'S INDUCING ANOTHER MEMORY!
BUT... NOT A MEMORY OF KOBOL. THAT'S DEEP SPACE!
STARBUCK, THAT ASTEROID ISN'T SCANNING PROPERLY!
AND NO WONDER! IT'S A SHIELD FOR A CYLON PATROL!
HIT YOUR TURBOS AND LET'S GET OUT OF HERE!
BUT WHY, APOLLO? WE COULD USE SOME ACTION!
BESIDES, OUR INITIAL VOLLEY DESTROYED HALF OF 'EM!
DON'T ARGUE! THERE MUST BE A BASE SHIP IN THE VICINITY!
WE'RE ACTUALLY SEEING FATHER'S THOUGHTS--A VISION FROM HIS PAST!
A VISION--OR A NIGHTMARE?!

COMMANDER, BLUE SQUADRON REPORTS A CYLON ENCOUNTER.

AS WE EXPECTED, EH, COLONEL?

YET, STRANGE REPORTS OF UNEXPLAINABLE SIGHTINGS HAVE BEEN FILTERING INTO THE COLONIES FROM THIS GALACTIC SECTOR, WELL, TIGH? DO YOU THINK THEY'RE ALL DUE TO INCREASED CYLON ACTIVITY?

WHAT ELSE, ADAMA? SURELY, YOU DON'T BELIEVE THOSE WILD TALES OF A SPACE MONSTER!

NO, AND YET...

COMMANDER! I HAVE A STRANGE BLIP ON THE LONG-RANGE SCANNER! IDENTIFICATION IS IMPOSSIBLE AT THIS DISTANCE-- BUT THE THING IS INCREDIBLY HUGE!

TRANSMIT THE CO-ORDINATES TO BLUE SQUADRON.

FATHER, WHAT... WHAT DO YOU SUPPOSE IT IS?

POSSIBLY A NEW CYLON WEAPON, ZAC. WE NEED TO INVESTIGATE IMMEDIATELY. THAT'S WHY I'M SENDING YOUR OLDER BROTHER AND STARBUCK ON...

...ANOTHER MISSION! FRAK!

SOMETHING WRONG, STARBUCK?

A VERY WARM SPACE SIREN AWAITS MY FORM AT THE OFFICERS CLUB.

RELAX. A FEW AMBROSIAS CAN ONLY MAKE HER MORE RECEPTIVE.

THIS YOU SAY TO A MAN IN LOVE!

CENTONS LATER...

APOLLO, SOMETHING'S WRONG! MY SCANNER'S GOING CRAZY!

LT. STARBUCK

GREAT CAPRICA!

APOLLO

STARBUCK, YOUR SCANNER'S FINE. JUST LOOK...

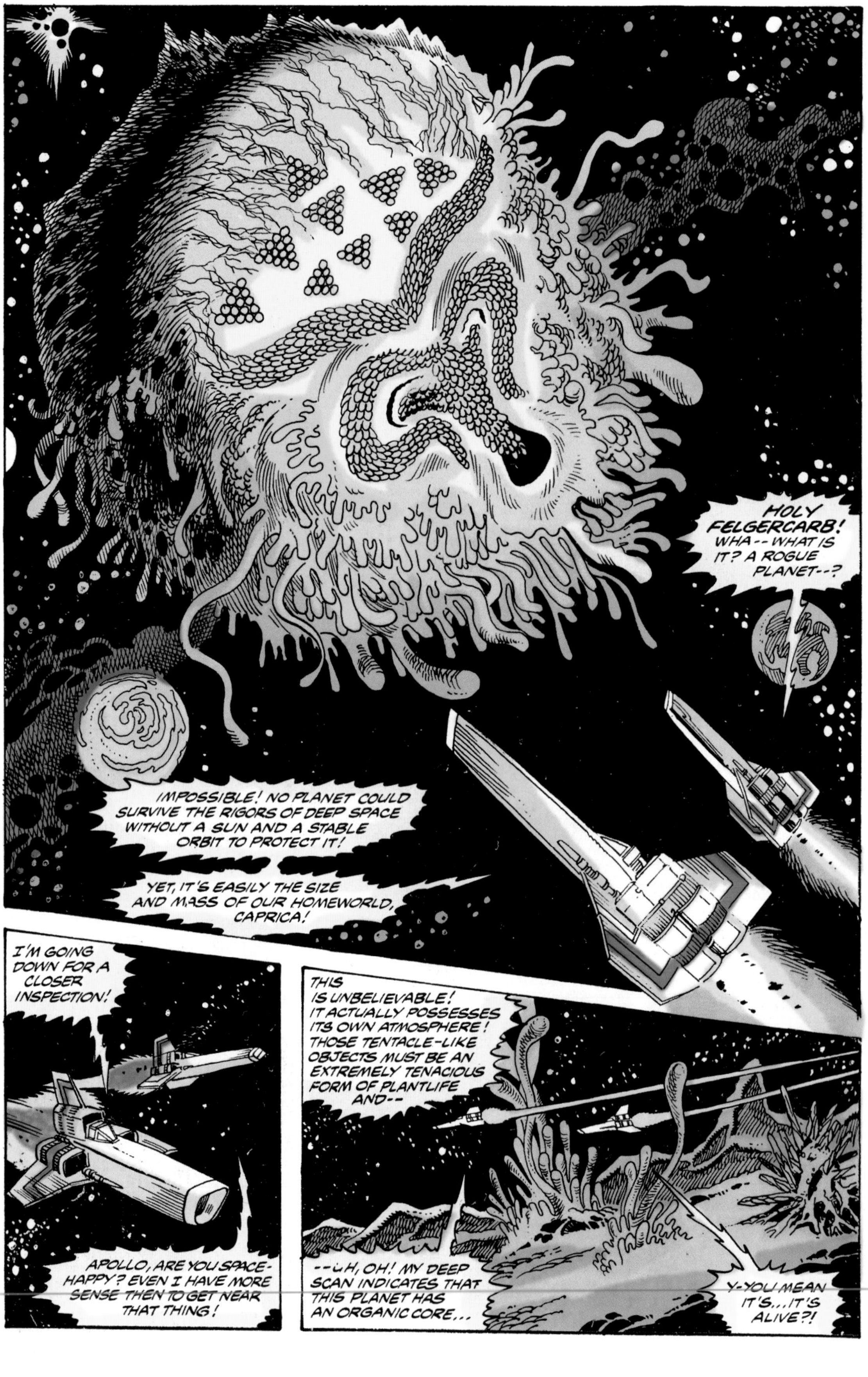
HOLY FELGERCARB! WHA-- WHAT IS IT? A ROGUE PLANET--?
IMPOSSIBLE! NO PLANET COULD SURVIVE THE RIGORS OF DEEP SPACE WITHOUT A SUN AND A STABLE ORBIT TO PROTECT IT!
YET, IT'S EASILY THE SIZE AND MASS OF OUR HOMEWORLD, CAPRICA!
I'M GOING DOWN FOR A CLOSER INSPECTION!
APOLLO, ARE YOU SPACE-HAPPY? EVEN I HAVE MORE SENSE THEN TO GET NEAR THAT THING!
THIS IS UNBELIEVABLE! IT ACTUALLY POSSESSES ITS OWN ATMOSPHERE! THOSE TENTACLE-LIKE OBJECTS MUST BE AN EXTREMELY TENACIOUS FORM OF PLANTLIFE AND--
--UH, OH! MY DEEP SCAN INDICATES THAT THIS PLANET HAS AN ORGANIC CORE...
Y-YOU MEAN IT'S... IT'S ALIVE?!

MAYBE, BUT OUR EQUIPMENT CAN'T MAKE THAT JUDGMENT WITH ANY CERTAINTY!

WHAT'S YOUR PLAN?

WE FOLLOW PROCEDURE AND IMPLANT THE PLANETOID WITH BIO-RECORDERS!

ODD! TOUCH-DOWN WAS EASY...ALMOST TOO EASY. THE GROUND DIDN'T SEEM THIS LEVEL ON MY INITIAL PASS.

IT'S ALMOST LIKE THE PLANET ITSELF CLEARED A RUNWAY FOR ME...

BUT THAT'S ABSURD!

STILL, EVERYTHING ABOUT THIS PLACE DEFIES LOGIC...

THOSE WEIRD APPENDAGES, SOME OF WHICH STRETCH FOR THOUSANDS OF MILES...THE HIGH OXYGEN CONTENT...THE GRAVITY...

ENGROSSED IN HIS THOUGHTS, APOLLO FAILS TO NOTICE THE PLANT-LIKE STALKS BEHIND HIM...

LIKE SENTIENT, SERPENTINE TRUNKS, THEY SLITHER FORWARD...

Y'KNOW, I MAY USE THIS PLACE FOR AN OCCASIONAL ROMANTIC INTERLUDE. THE RIFFRAFF WON'T COME HERE...

YES, THIS PLACE HAS DEFINITE POSSIBILITIES. I...

APOLLO, BEHIND YOU! THE PLANTS--!

THEY'RE ATTACKING!

*Before Apollo can react, he is completely enveloped within the slimy folds of alien flesh and...*

*;COUGH; ;COUGH;*
GAS -- I CAN'T BREATH!

DOWN, BUDDY! *GET DOWN!*

AND I'LL SKRAG 'EM AT THE STEM!

ERASE MY EARLIER COMMENTS. THE LADIES WOULDN'T APPRECIATE THIS PLACE -- TOO MUCH GROPING!

STARBUCK, I...

FORGET IT! BESIDES, IF ANYTHING HAPPENED TO YOU, I'D HAVE TO START PAYING FOR MY OWN DRINKS.

NOW LET'S PLANT THE RECORDERS --

-- AND GET THE FRAK OUT OF HERE!

*While aboard the galactica...*

BLUE SQUADRON IS TO RETURN IMMEDIATELY! ACCORDING TO THE INTELLIGENCE ALREADY TRANSMITTED TO OUR COMPUTERS, THAT PLANETOID IS ACTUALLY A LIVING CREATURE --

-- AND, IT'S HEADED OUR WAY!!!!

THE STARTLING NEWS GALVANIZES THE BATTLE-STAR INTO ACTION! ALL LEAVES ARE CANCELLED AS THE SHIP GOES ON A FULL ALERT...

SPECIAL PREPARATIONS ARE MADE FOR THE RETURNING WARRIORS...

A TOUR IN THE DECONTAMINATION WARD-- JUST WHAT I NEED!

ONCE HIS VIPER IS SONICALLY STERILIZED, APOLLO IS GREETED BY A MED-TECH AND HIS BROTHER ZAC...

WE'RE ALREADY IMMUNIZED AGAINST POSSIBLE CONTAMINATION, BUT THIS INNOCULATION SHOT SHOULD HOLD YOU UNTIL THE DECON CHAMBERS ARRIVE!

APOLLO, TELL ME ABOUT THAT 'PLANET'!

LATER, ZAC. AFTER DEBRIEFING.

THE BIO-TECHS WENT WHACKO ONCE THE RECORDERS BEGAN TRANSMITTING, THE CREATURE DEFIES CLASSIFICATION!

C'MON, STARBUCK! OPEN UP! THIS WON'T HURT A...

IIYEEEEEE!!!...

THAT SCREAM! SOMETHING'S WRONG...

YOUR FACE, STARBUCK! MY GOD, YOUR FACE--!

WHAT'S WITH YOU GUYS?

IS THIS A GAG?

TELL ME IT'S A GAG! PLEASE...

*BUT, BEFORE ANOTHER WORD CAN BE UTTERED...*

*THE MED-TECHS-- THEY'RE COLLAPSING!*

APOLLO, WHA- WHAT'S HAPPENING? MY SKIN FEELS LIKE IT'S AFLAME! I--I...

ZAC--?

*APOLLO LOOKS ON IN HORROR...*

*...AS HE WITNESSES HIS BROTHER'S GRISLY TRANSFORMATION...*

*...HEARS THE ANGUISHED CRIES OF HIS HIDEOUSLY STRICKEN CREWMEN...AND, REALIZES THAT SOMEHOW, SOME WAY, HE'S THE **CAUSE** OF IT ALL...*

*LATER, ON THE GALACTICA'S BRIDGE...*

ARE YOU CERTAIN THE CREATURE IS VEERING TOWARD US?

THERE CAN BE NO DOUBT!

COMMANDER ADAMA--!

THE PLAGUE IS RAPIDLY SPREADING THROUGHOUT THE SHIP!

ALL EFFORTS TO CONTAIN IT HAVE FAILED, AND...

...THE DISEASE APPEARS TO BE TRANSMITTED... TELEPATHICALLY!

WHAT--?

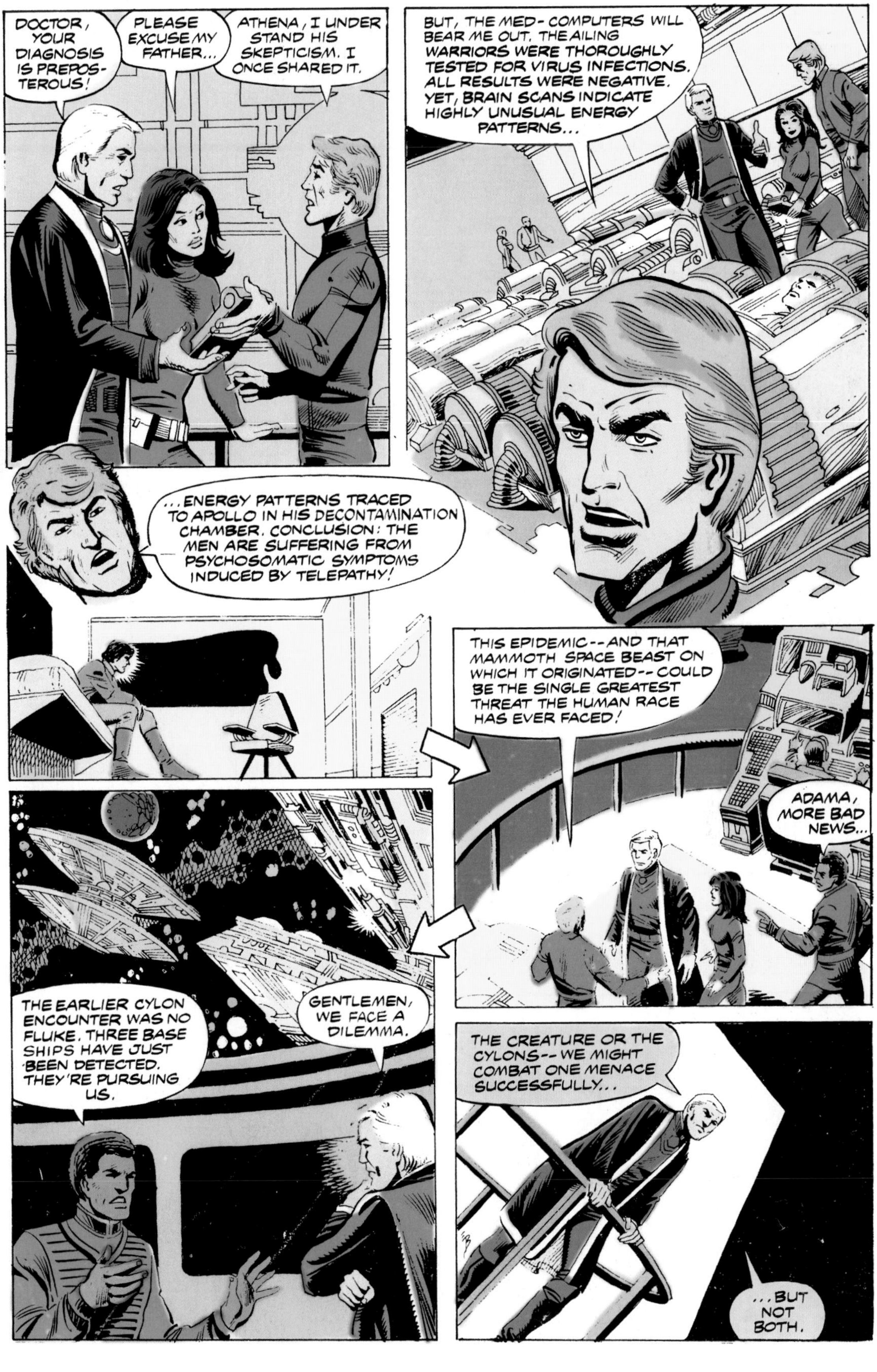
DOCTOR, YOUR DIAGNOSIS IS PREPOSTEROUS!
PLEASE EXCUSE MY FATHER...
ATHENA, I UNDERSTAND HIS SKEPTICISM. I ONCE SHARED IT.
BUT, THE MED-COMPUTERS WILL BEAR ME OUT. THE AILING WARRIORS WERE THOROUGHLY TESTED FOR VIRUS INFECTIONS. ALL RESULTS WERE NEGATIVE. YET, BRAIN SCANS INDICATE HIGHLY UNUSUAL ENERGY PATTERNS...
...ENERGY PATTERNS TRACED TO APOLLO IN HIS DECONTAMINATION CHAMBER. CONCLUSION: THE MEN ARE SUFFERING FROM PSYCHOSOMATIC SYMPTOMS INDUCED BY TELEPATHY!
THIS EPIDEMIC--AND THAT MAMMOTH SPACE BEAST ON WHICH IT ORIGINATED--COULD BE THE SINGLE GREATEST THREAT THE HUMAN RACE HAS EVER FACED!
ADAMA, MORE BAD NEWS...
THE EARLIER CYLON ENCOUNTER WAS NO FLUKE. THREE BASE SHIPS HAVE JUST BEEN DETECTED. THEY'RE PURSUING US.
GENTLEMEN, WE FACE A DILEMMA.
THE CREATURE OR THE CYLONS--WE MIGHT COMBAT ONE MENACE SUCCESSFULLY...
...BUT NOT BOTH.

JUST THEN, IN A CHILLED LONELY ROOM, HIS BODY TWISTED, HIS MIND RAVAGED, APOLLO STRUGGLES. AND THE DREAMS COME...

LIKE SOME MONSTROUS, CARNIVOROUS SPIDER, IT SQUATS AT THE EDGE OF THE UNIVERSE... CALLING, PLEADING, HUNGERING...

ONLY APOLLO CAN EASE ITS TORMENT. HIS MIND...IT DESIRES HIS MIND!

WITH A GHASTLY CRY, HE IS AWAKE...

...AND, HE KNOWS...

...KNOWS WHAT THE CREATURE CRAVES...

...KNOWS WHAT MUST BE DONE...

HE REACTS ACCORDINGLY...

WHILE... THE GALACTICA WILL CHANNEL ALL ITS RESOURCES, SIPHON ALL ITS ENERGY INTO ONE FURIOUS BLAST.

WE SHALL DESTROY THAT CREATURE!

NO! WITHOUT THE BEAST, WE'VE NO HOPE OF CURING THE PLAGUE!

ADAMA, THE POWER DRAIN WILL LEAVE US HELPLESS BEFORE THE CYLONS!

WE HAVE NO CHOICE IN THIS MATTER. IF THAT CREATURE SHOULD REACH THE COLONIES-- OUR CIVILIZATION WILL DIE!

MY DECISION STANDS!

MEANWHILE...

CAPTAIN APOLLO! THE PLAGUE HAS DRIVEN HIM MAD--!

HEY! YOU SHOULD BE IN SICK BAY!

SILENCE! NONE MAY BAR MY PATH!

ER...WHATEVER YOU SAY, PAL!

GOT TO STOP HIM BEFORE HE INFECTS THE WHOLE SHIP!

GENTLE DOWN, BUDDY! YOU'RE GOING BACK TO QUARANTINE!

NO!

NOTHING MUST STOP ME! NOTHING!

WITHIN MICRON, HE REACHES THE LAUNCHING BAY...

...AND...

COMMANDER, AN UNAUTHORIZED VIPER IS ON A COLLISION COURSE WITH THE SPACE BEAST!

WHAT--? WHO IS THE PILOT?

APOLLO.

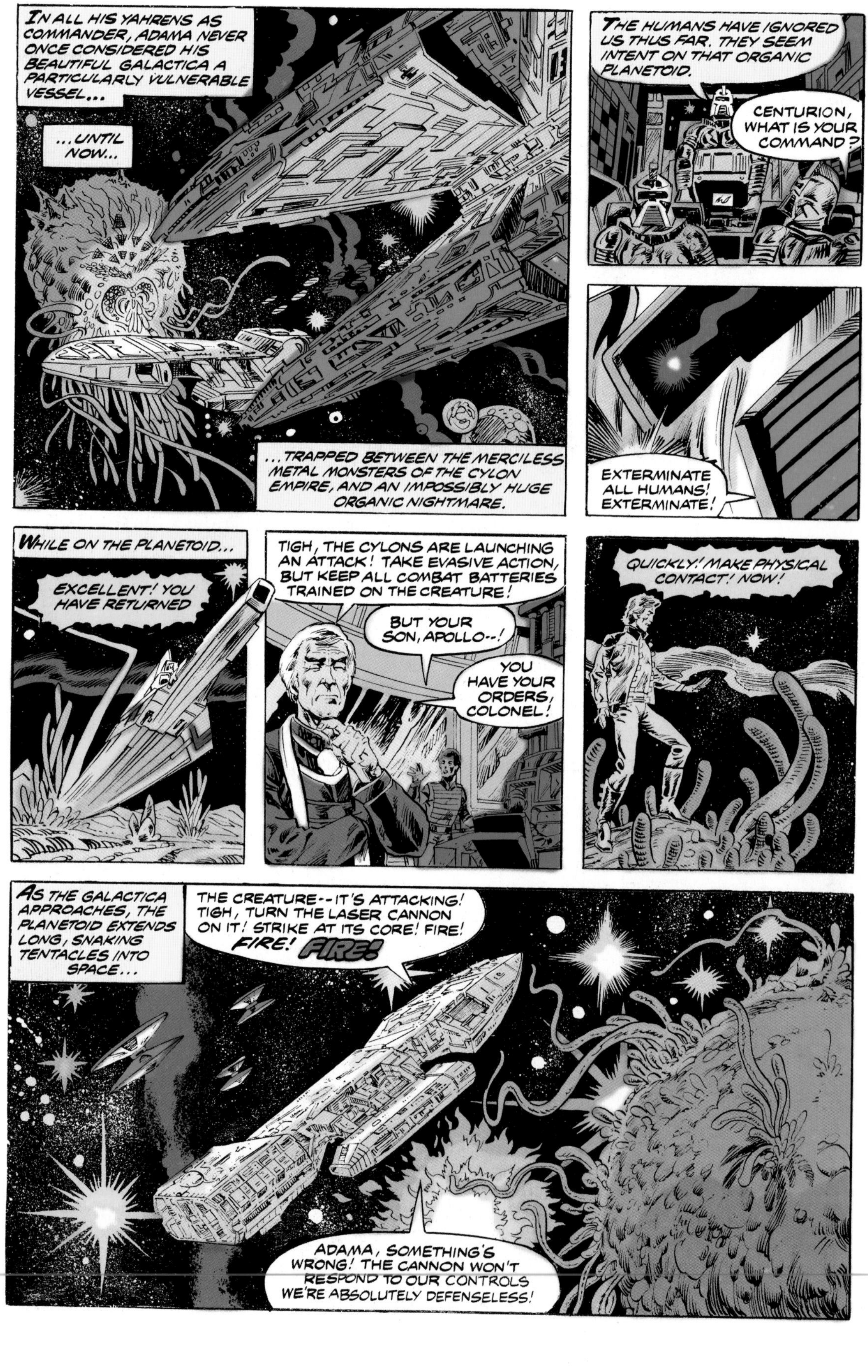
IN ALL HIS YAHRENS AS COMMANDER, ADAMA NEVER ONCE CONSIDERED HIS BEAUTIFUL GALACTICA A PARTICULARLY VULNERABLE VESSEL...
...UNTIL NOW...
...TRAPPED BETWEEN THE MERCILESS METAL MONSTERS OF THE CYLON EMPIRE, AND AN IMPOSSIBLY HUGE ORGANIC NIGHTMARE.
THE HUMANS HAVE IGNORED US THUS FAR. THEY SEEM INTENT ON THAT ORGANIC PLANETOID.
CENTURION, WHAT IS YOUR COMMAND?
EXTERMINATE ALL HUMANS! EXTERMINATE!
WHILE ON THE PLANETOID...
EXCELLENT! YOU HAVE RETURNED
TIGH, THE CYLONS ARE LAUNCHING AN ATTACK! TAKE EVASIVE ACTION, BUT KEEP ALL COMBAT BATTERIES TRAINED ON THE CREATURE!
BUT YOUR SON, APOLLO--!
YOU HAVE YOUR ORDERS, COLONEL!
QUICKLY! MAKE PHYSICAL CONTACT! NOW!
AS THE GALACTICA APPROACHES, THE PLANETOID EXTENDS LONG, SNAKING TENTACLES INTO SPACE...
THE CREATURE--IT'S ATTACKING! TIGH, TURN THE LASER CANNON ON IT! STRIKE AT ITS CORE! FIRE! FIRE! FIRE!
ADAMA, SOMETHING'S WRONG! THE CANNON WON'T RESPOND TO OUR CONTROLS WE'RE ABSOLUTELY DEFENSELESS!

TENTACLES, MONSTROUS AND DEADLY, LASH TOWARD THE BATTLESTAR! HEARTLESS CYLONS SWARM ABOUT HER, AND...

NONE OF OUR ARMAMENT IS FUNCTIONING! IT'S AS IF SOMETHING... SOME OUTSIDE FORCE--HAS RENDERED-- OUR INSTRUMENTATION USELESS!

WE WON'T GO DOWN WITHOUT A FIGHT!

SCRAMBLE THE VIPERS!

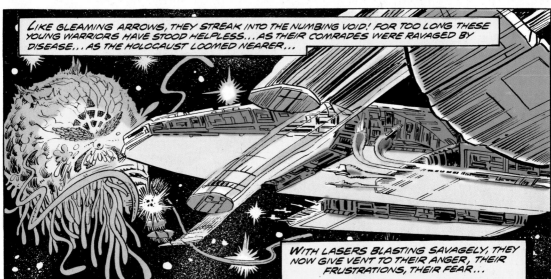

LIKE GLEAMING ARROWS, THEY STREAK INTO THE NUMBING VOID! FOR TOO LONG THESE YOUNG WARRIORS HAVE STOOD HELPLESS...AS THEIR COMRADES WERE RAVAGED BY DISEASE...AS THE HOLOCAUST LOOMED NEARER...

WITH LASERS BLASTING SAVAGELY, THEY NOW GIVE VENT TO THEIR ANGER, THEIR FRUSTRATIONS, THEIR FEAR...

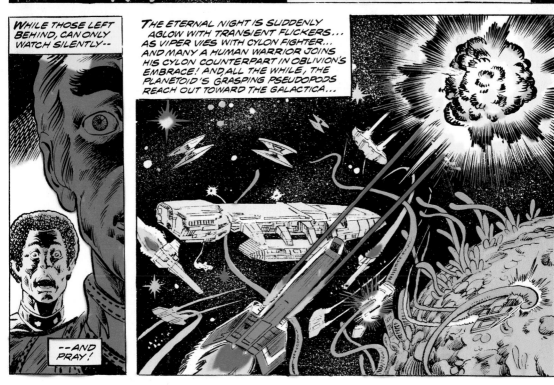

WHILE THOSE LEFT BEHIND, CAN ONLY WATCH SILENTLY--

--AND PRAY!

THE ETERNAL NIGHT IS SUDDENLY AGLOW WITH TRANSIENT FLICKERS... AS VIPER VIES WITH CYLON FIGHTER... AND MANY A HUMAN WARRIOR JOINS HIS CYLON COUNTERPART IN OBLIVION'S EMBRACE! AND ALL THE WHILE, THE PLANETOID'S GRASPING PSEUDOPODS REACH OUT TOWARD THE GALACTICA...

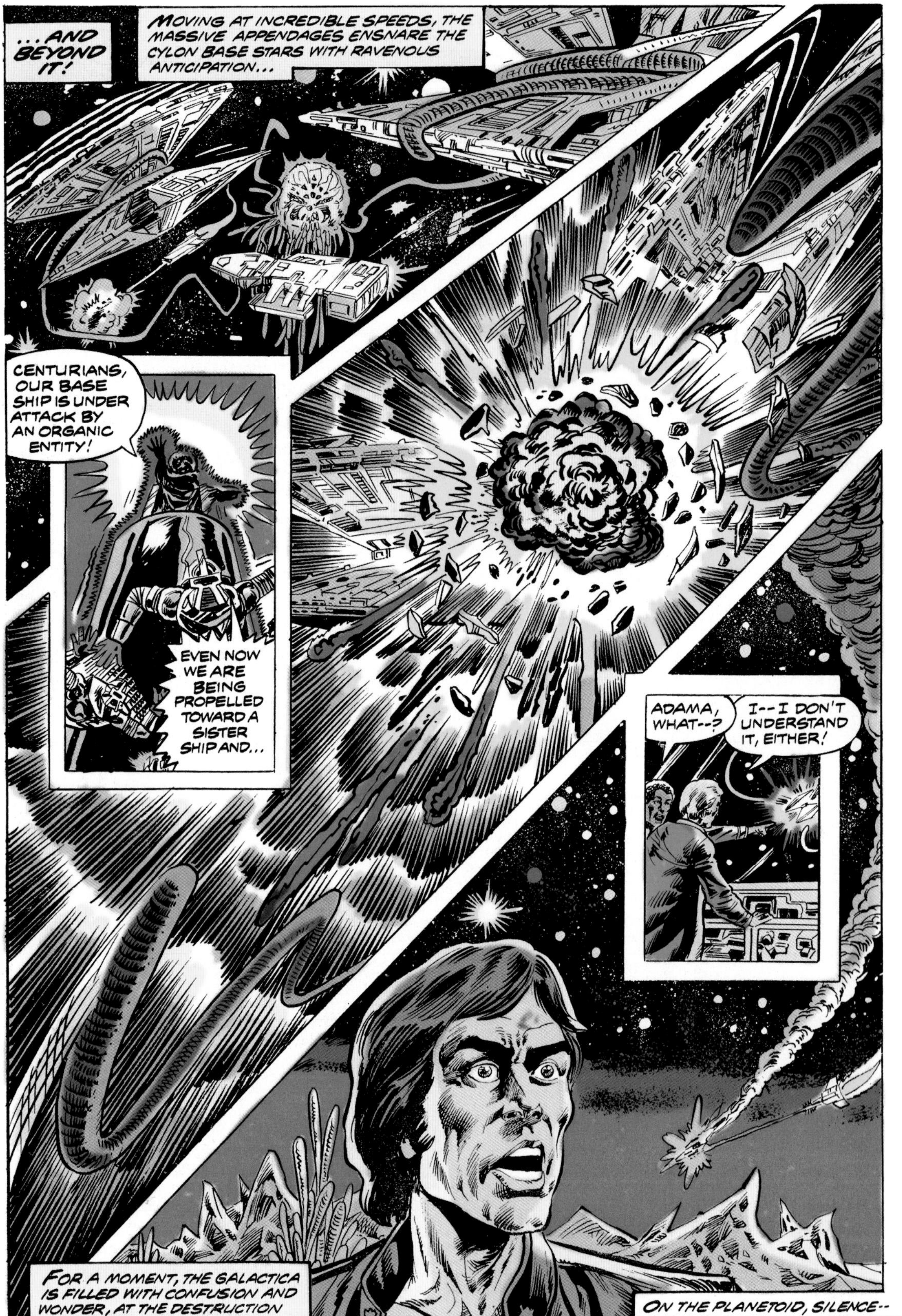
...AND BEYOND IT!
MOVING AT INCREDIBLE SPEEDS, THE MASSIVE APPENDAGES ENSNARE THE CYLON BASE STARS WITH RAVENOUS ANTICIPATION...
CENTURIANS, OUR BASE SHIP IS UNDER ATTACK BY AN ORGANIC ENTITY!
EVEN NOW WE ARE BEING PROPELLED TOWARD A SISTER SHIP AND...
ADAMA, WHAT--?
I--I DON'T UNDERSTAND IT, EITHER!
FOR A MOMENT, THE GALACTICA IS FILLED WITH CONFUSION AND WONDER, AT THE DESTRUCTION OF THE CYLON SHIPS. THEN THE CHEERS BEGIN...
ON THE PLANETOID, SILENCE--COLD AND UNYIELDING--REIGNS...

THE AIRTIGHT HULL OF THE FINAL CYLON WARSHIP IS SHATTERED BENEATH AN UNYIELDING TENTACLE...

COMMANDER, SCANNER REPORTS NO MORE CYLONS!

THE CREATURE-- IT SPANNED DEEP SPACE TO DESTROY THEM ALL! BUT HOW?

MY PHYSICAL MANIFESTATION IS DIMENSIONALLY TRANSCENDENTAL!

WHAT THE FRAK--?

GREETINGS, I AM "HE-WHO-SEARCHES-YET-SURVIVES"... THE PLANETOID WHOM YOU MISTAKENLY FEARED... THOUGH OUR ASPECTS ARE VASTLY DIFFERENT, WE ARE BROTHERS OF THE MIND AND SOUL... WHICH IS WHY I AIDED YOU AGAINST THOSE METAL ONES WHO DESIRE AN ABSENCE OF LIFE...

"COMMUNICATION BETWEEN SPECIES AS DIVERSE AS OURS IS DIFFICULT AT BEST... THE 'PLAGUE' YOUR PILOTS CONTRACTED FROM ME WAS MERELY THE FIRST STEP AT BRIDGING THE GAP... AND ITS SYMPTOMS WILL SOON VANISH...

"THE 'APOLLO-HE' IS TRANSMUTING MY THOUGHTS TO YOUR REALITY... HE WILL RETURN UNHARMED...

"WE HAVE MUCH TO LEARN FROM EACH OTHER...

"FOR UNTOLD MILLENNIA I HAVE EXPLORED THE STELLAR SEAS ALONE... NOW I HUNGER FOR COMPANIONSHIP... FOR DEEP SPACE IS THE LONELIEST PLACE OF ALL... AND YOUR PRESENCE WILL COMFORT ME FOR A BRIEF WHILE..."

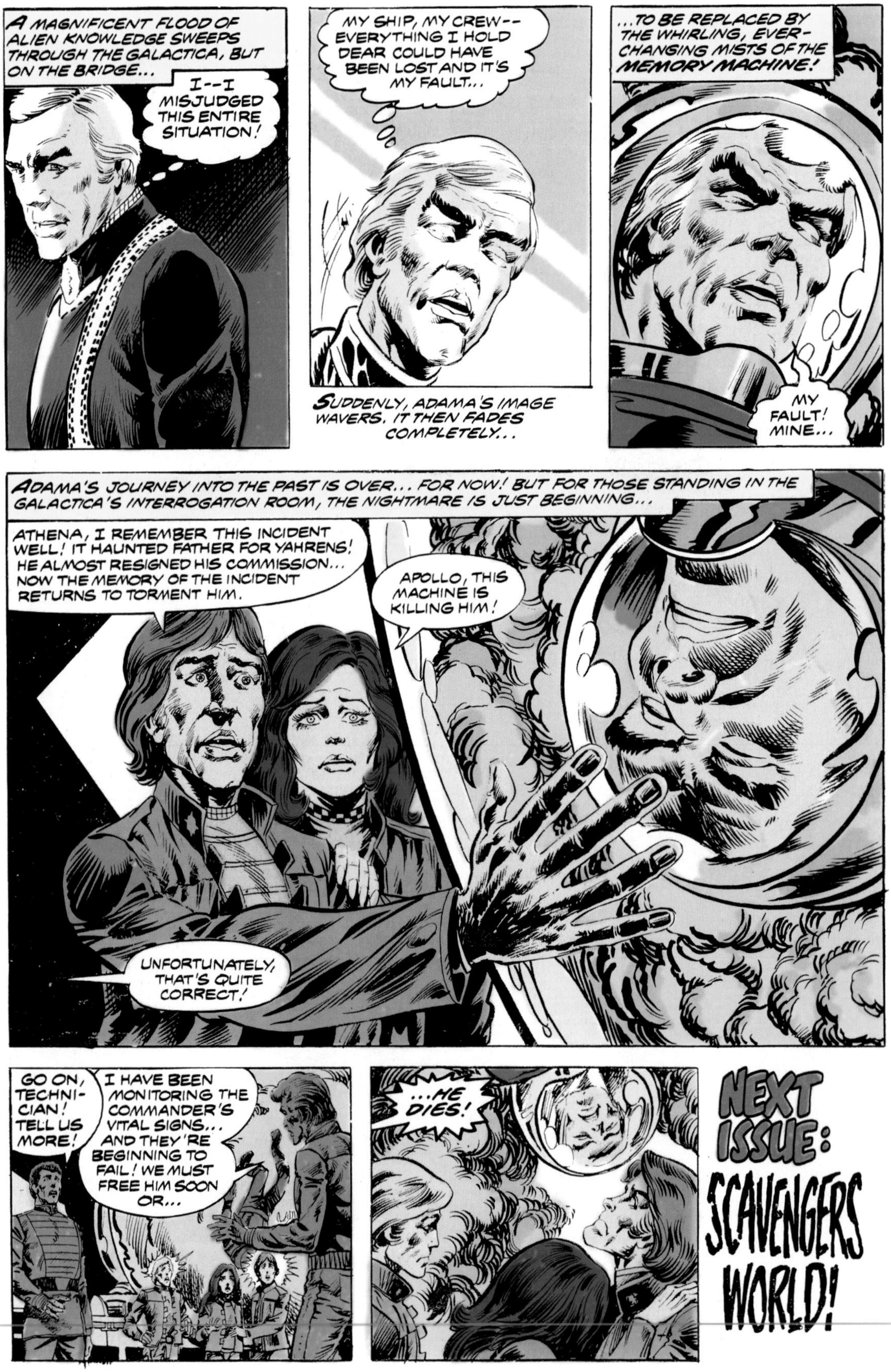

A MAGNIFICENT FLOOD OF ALIEN KNOWLEDGE SWEEPS THROUGH THE GALACTICA, BUT ON THE BRIDGE...
I--I MISJUDGED THIS ENTIRE SITUATION!
MY SHIP, MY CREW-- EVERYTHING I HOLD DEAR COULD HAVE BEEN LOST AND IT'S MY FAULT...
SUDDENLY, ADAMA'S IMAGE WAVERS. IT THEN FADES COMPLETELY...
...TO BE REPLACED BY THE WHIRLING, EVER-CHANGING MISTS OF THE MEMORY MACHINE!
MY FAULT! MINE...
ADAMA'S JOURNEY INTO THE PAST IS OVER... FOR NOW! BUT FOR THOSE STANDING IN THE GALACTICA'S INTERROGATION ROOM, THE NIGHTMARE IS JUST BEGINNING...
ATHENA, I REMEMBER THIS INCIDENT WELL! IT HAUNTED FATHER FOR YAHRENS! HE ALMOST RESIGNED HIS COMMISSION... NOW THE MEMORY OF THE INCIDENT RETURNS TO TORMENT HIM.
APOLLO, THIS MACHINE IS KILLING HIM!
UNFORTUNATELY, THAT'S QUITE CORRECT!
GO ON, TECHNICIAN! TELL US MORE!
I HAVE BEEN MONITORING THE COMMANDER'S VITAL SIGNS... AND THEY'RE BEGINNING TO FAIL! WE MUST FREE HIM SOON OR...
...HE DIES!
NEXT ISSUE:
SCAVENGERS WORLD!

There are those who believe life here began out there, far across the universe, with tribes of humans who may have been the forefathers of the Egyptians. Or the Toltecs. Or the Mayans. Some believe there may yet be brothers of man who even now fight to survive somewhere beyond the heavens!

# STan Lee PRESENTS: BattlestaR GALACTICA ™ ·

Based on the television series Battlestar Galactica™ · written and created by Glen Larson.

"COMMANDER'S LOG, ADDENDUM 138-14-06, COLONEL TIGH SPEAK-ING--DESPITE REPEATED PATROLS, WE HAVE FOUND NO TRACE OF THE AGRO-SHIP. OUR CHANCES OF EVER LOCATING IT, OR THE OTHER TWO MISSING VESSELS, ARE FADING AS RAPIDLY AS OUR DWINDLING FOOD RESERVES--"

"--AS THE FLEET CONTINUES TO DRIFT, LOST WITHIN THIS DAMNABLE AND SEEMINGLY ENDLESS VOID BETWEEN THE STARS.

"AND THE ONLY MAN WHO CAN HELP US ALSO CON-TINUES TO DRIFT, LOST WITHIN THE SEEMINGLY END-LESS VOID OF HIS OWN MEMORIES."

FATHER! WE HAVE TO DO SOMETHING, COLONEL TIGH!

THERE'S NOTHING WE CAN DO, APOLLO! SIRE URI'S GUARDS SABOTAGED THE MEMORY MACHINE--

--AND COMMANDER ADAMA IS TRAPPED INSIDE!

LG603

# SCAVENGE WORLD

**ROGER McKENZIE** & **WALTER SIMONSON**
SCRIPT - PLOT - LAYOUTS
**KLAUS JANSON** * *JIM NOVAK* * *BOB SHAREN*
FINISHES    LETTERER    COLORIST
**ALLEN MILGROM** * **JIM SHOOTER**
EDITOR    ED - IN - CHIEF

"HERE'S HOW IT HAPPENED..."

THERE'S STILL TIME TO RECONSIDER... SIR.

APOLLO, ATHENA ...MY CHILDREN ...I APPRECIATE YOUR CONCERN, BUT YOU BOTH KNOW THE ONE THING WE DO **NOT** HAVE IS TIME. MY MIND IS MADE UP...

"AND HIS MIND WAS STRIPPED BARE AS HE PLUNGED INTO THE COLD, CHEMICAL CONFINES OF THE MEMORY STIMULATOR, SEARCHING FOR A SINGLE THOUGHT, A BRIEFLY-GLIMPSED, ANCIENT INSCRIPTION--

"--THAT CHRONICLED THE MIGRATION OF THE 13TH, AND LAST, TRIBE OF MANKIND THAT HAD FLED THE DYING PLANET OF KOBOL, HOME PLANET OF THE ENTIRE HUMAN RACE.

"IF, WITH THE STIMULATOR'S AID, ADAMA COULD RECALL THE INSCRIPTION-- LEARN THE PATH ACROSS THE HEAVENS TO A COLONY NAMED EARTH--

"-- PERHAPS WE WOULD FIND **SANCTUARY** FROM CYLON OPPRESSION. AN END TO THE THOUSAND-YEAR WAR WITH THOSE HOSTILE, ROBOT BEINGS WHO LEFT US HOMELESS DESPERATE WANDERERS

THE IMAGE OF A CYLON RAIDER! WE CAN ACTUALLY **SEE** MY FATHER'S THOUGHTS!

"I WISH, NOW, WE HAD BEEN ABLE TO SEE SIRE URI'S DARK THOUGHTS, INSTEAD. BUT BEFORE ANYONE COULD STOP HIM, HE WRESTED CONTROL OF THE COUNCIL OF TWELVE, OUR RULING BODY, AWAY FROM ADAMA--

"--AND HAD USED HIS PERSONAL GUARDS TO ATTACK THE **COMMANDER!**

"NOW, THE COMMANDER IS LITERALLY DROWNING IN HIS OWN MEMORIES. WITHOUT PROPER SAFEGUARDS, WE DARE NOT REMOVE HIM FROM HIS SEA OF DREAMS.

ZZRAAAKK.

"THE TRAUMA OF PREMATURE AWAKENING WOULD SHATTER HIS MIND AS SURELY AS LASER-FIRE SHATTERED THE COMPUTER MONITORS OF THE MEMORY MACHINE."

URI, YOU BETTER PRAY MY FATHER DOESN'T DIE, OR--!

M-MY DEAR BOY,... BE REASONABLE! SURELY YOU DON'T THINK I--!

"URI, TO NO ONE'S SURPRISE, PLEADED INNOCENCE-- MAINTAINING THE ATTACK WAS INSTIGATED **WITH-OUT** HIS KNOWLEDGE.

IT HAS BEEN A WEEK, SHIP'S TIME, SINCE THE TRAGEDY. THE FLEET IS GROWING MORE RESTLESS WITH EACH PASSING CENTON...

...AND I HAVE NEVER FELT SO HELPLESS...

STATUS REPORT, ALPHA PATROL.

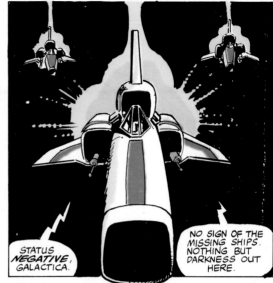

STATUS *NEGATIVE*, GALACTICA.

NO SIGN OF THE MISSING SHIPS. NOTHING BUT DARKNESS OUT HERE.

STARBUCK! BOOMER! LONG RANGE SCANNERS CAUGHT SOMETHING, JUST FOR A MICRON, THEN IT WAS GONE! I--!

THERE IT IS AGAIN! I'M NOT SURE, BUT--!

BUT IT COULD BE WHAT WE'RE LOOKING FOR, ATHENA! LOCK IN COORDINATES AND COMPUTE ESTIMATED RENDEZVOUS POINT TIMETABLE!

IMPOSSIBLE TO VECTOR E.R.P., STARBUCK. TOO MUCH STATIC.

FRAKKING VOID--! WE MIGHT AS WELL BE FLYING BLIND! ALL RIGHT, WE DO THIS THE HARD WAY! MANUAL SCAN, STEADY AS SHE GOES!

I'VE GOT SOMETHING, STARBUCK! DEAD AHEAD AND CLOSING FAST!

BUT... MY SCANNER'S GOING CRAZY! THESE READ-OUTS ARE IMPOSSIBLE!

BOOMER, YOU'D BETTER CONTACT THE GALACTICA...

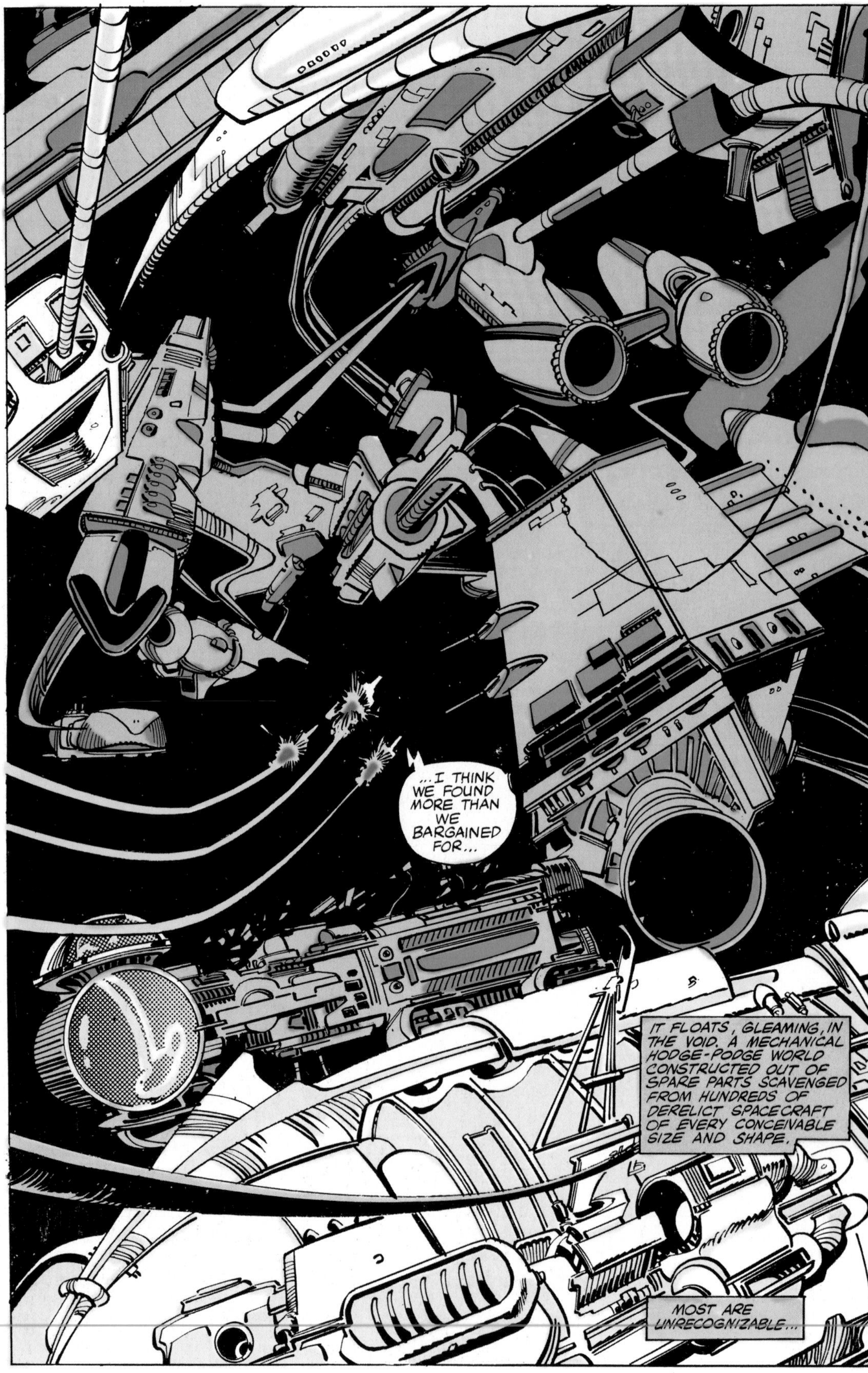
...I THINK WE FOUND MORE THAN WE BARGAINED FOR...
IT FLOATS, GLEAMING, IN THE VOID. A MECHANICAL HODGE-PODGE WORLD CONSTRUCTED OUT OF SPARE PARTS SCAVENGED FROM HUNDREDS OF DERELICT SPACECRAFT OF EVERY CONCEIVABLE SIZE AND SHAPE.
MOST ARE UNRECOGNIZABLE...

...ONE IS NOT.

THERE'S THE AGRO-SHIP! OR WHAT'S LEFT OF IT! IT'S BEING DIS-MANTLED!

BOOMER, HAVE YOU REACHED COLONEL TIGH YET? BOOMER?

STARBUCK! BOOMER CUT OFF HIS SHIP-TO-SHIP COMMUNI-CATIONS! BUT WHY WOULD HE--?

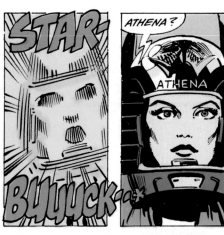

STAR-BUUUCK-a*

ATHENA?

ATHENA

HEY!

ATHENA? BOOMER? WHAT'S GOTTEN INTO YOU?

BREAKING FORMATION WITHOUT A WORD--

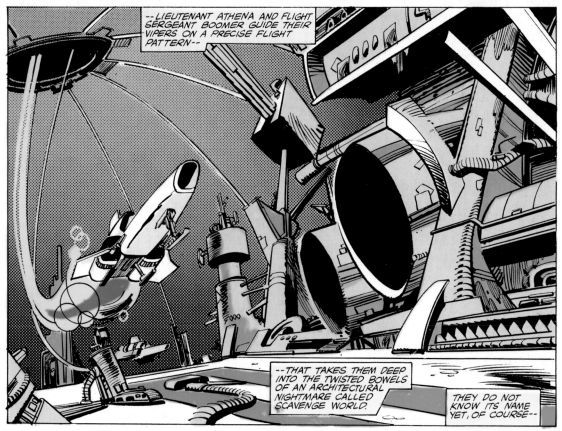

--LIEUTENANT ATHENA AND FLIGHT SERGEANT BOOMER GUIDE THEIR VIPERS ON A PRECISE FLIGHT PATTERN--

--THAT TAKES THEM DEEP INTO THE TWISTED BOWELS OF AN ARCHITECTURAL NIGHTMARE CALLED SCAVENGE WORLD.

THEY DO NOT KNOW ITS NAME YET, OF COURSE--

--BUT THEY WILL LEARN!

MORE PRETTIES FOR SCAVENGE WORLD!

NICE PRETTIES! SHINY PRETTIES!

THERE ARE... UGH... LIFE-FORMS, TOO!

UGLY BRUTE... BUT IT'S ZONKED!

TAKE IT AND THE OTHER TO EURAYLE! THAT'S THE DEAL! SHE GETS THE FLESH--

--WE GET THE SPARE PARTS!

THE PRETTIES!

WORM OF A WORM! LOOK! ANOTHER ONE!

OH, HAPPY DAY!

I SAW IT FIRST! I GET THE TRIM!

NO! ME! ME! ME!

THESE...THINGS... *AREN'T* CYLONS. SO WHERE'D THEY GET THE CYLON ARMOR?

ALL RIGHT, THAT'S FAR ENOUGH! JUST STAY BACK!

WHAT IS THIS PLACE? WHO ARE YOU? WHAT HAVE YOU DONE WITH MY FRIENDS?

SKRAAAK

NO FAIR! YOU'RE SUPPOSED TO BE ZONKED! WHERE ARE THE TAMERS?

HERE!

TAMERS?

WON'T TAKE LONG. NEVER DOES.

HOPE THIS ONE HAS BLOOD. LIKE BLOOD BEST.

BOOMER! ATHENA!

I COULD USE A HAND...

AND SPEAKING OF HANDS--

--HANDS OFF!

HOLD ON, YOU TWO! I'M--

--LOST...

WHICH WAY DID THEY GO?

SPLIT UP! SEARCH EVERY CORRIDOR!

IT CAN'T GET FAR!

THEY... WHATEVER THEY ARE,...ARE RIGHT BEHIND ME! AND THEY DON'T SEEM TO BE TOO FRIENDLY!

I'VE GOT TO DITCH 'EM... FAST!

HUH? WHAT'S THIS?

JACK-POT!

JACK-POT?!

THIS A PRIVATE GAME...

...OR CAN ANYONE PLAY?

PLUTAVARIAN THREE-SPOT, IS THE GAME, ISN'T IT?

WELL?

HOW'S THIS FOR OPENERS?

WHEW!

MEANWHILE, AS STARBUCK LOSES HIS PURSUERS AND WINS THE FIRST HAND...

CAPTAIN... SCANNERS PICKING UP INCOMING CRAFT... CLOSING AT ATTACK SPEED!

MUST BE A CYLON PATROL! THEY'VE FOUND US! GET COLONEL TIGH UP HERE ON THE DOUBLE -- AND SOUND RED ALERT!

THAT WON'T BE NECESSARY, CAPTAIN!

YOU SEEM TO HAVE FORGOTTEN WHO GIVES THE ORDERS HERE. AND MY ORDERS ARE TO WAIT.

IF THIS IS MERELY ALPHA PATROL, RETURNING WITH THE MISSING SHIPS, I SEE NO REASON TO THROW THE ENTIRE FLEET INTO A STATE OF PANIC.

AND IF IT'S *NOT* ALPHA PATROL, WHAT DO WE DO THEN, URI?

WHAT DO WE DO NOW, SIR?

THE GALACTICA IS UNDER DIRECT CYLON ATTACK!

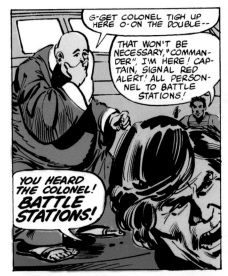

G-GET COLONEL TIGH UP HERE O-ON THE DOUBLE--

THAT WON'T BE NECESSARY, "COMMANDER", I'M HERE! CAPTAIN, SIGNAL RED ALERT! ALL PERSONNEL TO BATTLE STATIONS!

YOU HEARD THE COLONEL! BATTLE STATIONS!

HELMSMAN! KEEP THE GALACTICA *BETWEEN* THE CYLON RAIDERS AND THE REST OF THE FLEET AT ALL COSTS!

AYE, COLONEL!

READY LASER TURRETS! AT MY ORDER--

FIRE!

ALL ENGINES AHEAD FULL!

WE'RE GONNA *RAM* 'EM!

CENTURIAN SCOUTS TO BASESHIP! INFORM LUCIFER WE HAVE FOUND THE HUMANS!

SCRAMBLE ALL AVAILABLE RAIDERS TO CO-ORDINATES--!

SHRAAAK

 MEANWHILE, ACTION OF A DIFFERENT SORT IS TAKING PLACE BACK AT THE GAMING TABLES OF SCAVENGE WORLD...

YOUR BET, PAL. YOU IN OR OUT?

 IN.

 I TRUST MY ENSIGNIA OF RANK WILL SUFFICIENTLY COVER YOUR WAGER.

 B-BUT, GENERAL TRAGG...

 READ 'EM AND WEEP PAL! A PERFECT PLERD!

 A PER... PER... PERFECT...

OH, NO! I-- I'M RUINED...

 GENTLEMEN, IT'S BEEN A REAL PLEASURE!

 BUT I REALLY MUST BE--

RUINED...

 --GO--OH--!

HI, GUYS, GUESS YOU BEEN LOOKIN' FOR ME, HUH?

LATER, IN A DINGY PRISON CELL...

--THEN I JUST... WENT BLANK. NEXT THING I KNEW I WOKE UP HERE...

...WHEREVER 'HERE' IS. WONDER WHAT HAPPENED TO STARBUCK?

I WISH I KNEW, BOOMER. HOPE HE'S NOT IN TROUBLE, I --UH, OH--! WE'VE GOT COMPANY!

YOU ARE TO COME WITH ME...

...GENERAL'S ORDERS!

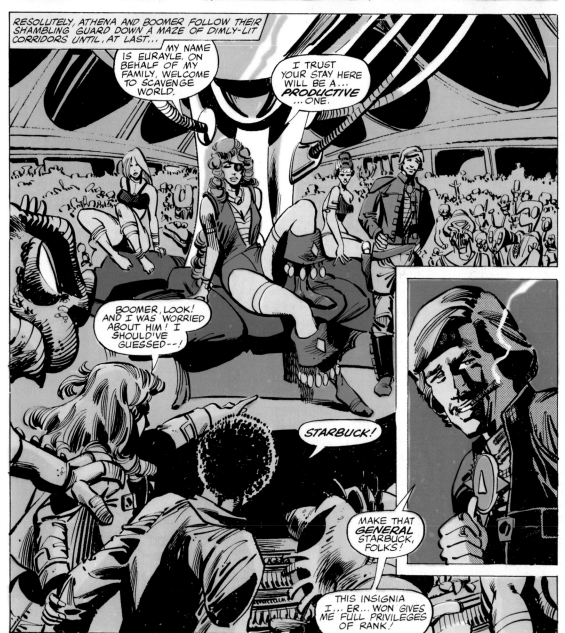

RESOLUTELY, ATHENA AND BOOMER FOLLOW THEIR SHAMBLING GUARD DOWN A MAZE OF DIMLY-LIT CORRIDORS UNTIL, AT LAST...

MY NAME IS EURAYLE. ON BEHALF OF MY FAMILY, WELCOME TO SCAVENGE WORLD.

I TRUST YOUR STAY HERE WILL BE A... PRODUCTIVE ...ONE.

BOOMER, LOOK! AND I WAS WORRIED ABOUT HIM! I SHOULD'VE GUESSED--!

STARBUCK!

MAKE THAT GENERAL STARBUCK, FOLKS!

THIS INSIGNIA I... ER... WON GIVES ME FULL PRIVILEGES OF RANK!

YOUR FRIENDS WILL MAKE EXCELLENT FAMILY MEMBERS, STARBUCK. AT LEAST, UNLIKE YOURSELF, THEY ARE EASILY MIND-CONTROLLED... WHICH IS HOW WE CAUSED THEM TO FLY HERE.

YEAH, WELL WE *ALL* GOT OUR FAULTS, Y'KNOW?

LEMME HANDLE THIS, OK?

*STARBUCK--!*

SSSHH--! LISTEN, WE'RE IN A REAL JAM! BUT DON'T WORRY, I HAVE A PLAN!

STARBUCK, I DO NOT LIKE WHISPERING. THERE ARE NO SECRETS ON SCAVENGE WORLD.

THERE IS ONLY UNITY, AS PRESCRIBED BY OUR ANCESTORS EONS AGO WHEN THEY FOUNDED SCAVENGE WORLD. THEY, LIKE YOU, WERE WANDERERS LOST AND EVENTUALLY DRAWN HERE TO THE MAGNETIC CENTER OF THE VOID.

SOME OF US WERE *FORCED* HERE!

DON'T ANTAGONIZE HER, BOOMER!

WE ARE SCAVENGERS. WE NEED SPARE PARTS TO INSURE OUR CONTINUED EXISTENCE.

YOU'VE SEEN OUR WORLD. AND WHILE IT IS TRUE YOU *WERE* LURED HERE, STILL YOU ARE WELCOMED WITH OPEN ARMS. YOU AND THE REST OF YOUR FLEET.

APPARENTLY, YOU CAN *READ* MINDS AS WELL AS *CONTROL* THEM, EURAYLE. BUT IF YOU KNOW ABOUT OUR FLEET--

--THEN YOU KNOW OUR NUMBERS ARE FEW AND OUR SHIPS MOSTLY DERELICTS. AND YOU PROBABLY ALSO KNOW WE'RE RUNNING FROM THE CYLONS.

JUDGING FROM SOME OF THE HARDWARE I'VE SEEN AROUND HERE YOU'VE ALREADY MET THEM.

I'VE GOT A DEAL FOR YOU, EURAYLE. YOU HELP US ESCAPE THIS VOID, AND WE'LL DELIVER YOU ENOUGH CYLONS TO BUILD A WHOLE NEW SCAVENGE WORLD IF YOU LIKE!

EURAYLE...

BESIDES, CYLONS ARE ONE HUNDRED PERCENT GUARANTEED SPARE PARTS!

HMMM... IT *IS* AN INTERESTING PROPOSITION, STARBUCK...

B-BUT EURAYLE...

THEN IT'S A DEAL?

DEAL!

EURAYLE, *LOOK...*

LOOK! THE HUMANS' *FLEET!* THEY HAVE ARRIVED!

ALL THE PRETTIES! SO VERY MANY PRETTIES!

THE HUMAN LIED! HE SAID THERE WAS ONLY A FEW SHIPS! HE LIED! HE LIED!

STARBUCK!

WELL... ...A DEAL'S A DEAL.

RIGHT?

HAHAHAHAHAHAHA HAHAHA

STARBUCK, YOU *CON!* YOU'D *GO* PLACES ON SCAVENGE WORLD! THERE'S NOTHING I LIKE BETTER THAN A MAN WHO LIVES BY HIS WITS!

WELL, HEHHEH, I TRY...

ATHENA, HOW IS IT STARBUCK WASN'T MIND-CONTROLLED?

IT ONLY WORKS ON A MIND WITH AN I.Q. HIGHER THAN A DAGGIT'S!

AND, AS THE COLONIAL FLEET REACHES SCAVENGE WORLD...

BRING HER ABOUT, HELMSMAN! WE'RE GETTING OUT OF HERE!

NOT WITHOUT THE REST OF THE FLEET WE'RE NOT! YOU TRIED ABANDONING THEM ONCE BEFORE, URI. IT DIDN'T WORK THEN.

AND IT WON'T WORK NOW.

OUR DUTY IS TO PROTECT THE FLEET. AND THAT'S JUST WHAT WE'LL DO!

CAPTAIN! MESSAGE COMING IN-- FROM LIEUTENANT STARBUCK!

SHORTLY...

THAT'S ABOUT IT, CAPTAIN! OUR MISSING SHIPS AND CREW-MEMBERS WILL BE RETURNED TO US AND WE'LL BE GIVEN SAFE PASSAGE FROM THE VOID.

IN RETURN WE HAVE TO LURE THE CYLONS INTO A TRAP HERE AT SCAVENGE WORLD.

"THAT WON'T BE DIFFICULT, STARBUCK. WE...AH... RAN INTO A CYLON PATROL EARLIER, OTHERS PROBABLY AREN'T FAR BEHIND."

"UH, APOLLO, HOW'S COMMANDER ADAMA? IS HE--?"

HE'S STILL ALIVE, STARBUCK, AND HE'S STILL TRAPPED IN THE MEMORY STIMULATOR. DOCTOR WILKER AND DOCTOR SPANG HAVE DONE EVERYTHING THEY CAN--

--BUT MY FATHER MAY NEVER BE FREED FROM THE PRISON OF HIS OWN MEMORIES.

I'VE GOT A DEAL FOR YOU, CAPTAIN.

I HAVE CERTAIN... UH... ABILITIES. I BELIEVE I CAN HELP YOUR FATHER.

AND IN RETURN FOR HIS LIFE, ALL I ASK IS...

...STARBUCK!

THAT SEEMS A FAIR TRADE. A COMMANDER... FOR A GENERAL.

NEXT: FAREWELL TO HARMS!

# #12

"THE TRAP!"

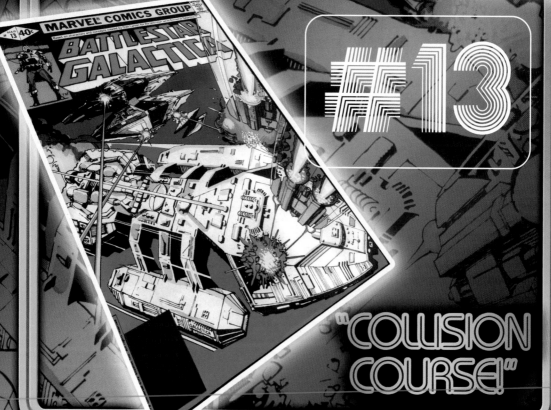

# #13

"COLLISION COURSE!"

# STaN Lee PRESENTS: BattlestaR GALACTICA™ •

Based on the television series Battlestar Galactica™ • written and created by Glen Larson.

WELL, STARBUCK, THIS IS *ANOTHER* FINE MESS YOU'VE GOTTEN US INTO!

LF634

# THE TRAP!

ROGER McKENZIE & WALT SIMONSON
writer/co-plotters/penciler
KLAUS JANSON / COSTANZA / DOC MARTIN
inker / letterer / colorist
ALLEN MILGROM & JIM SHOOTER
editors

ME? *ME?!* NOW LISTEN, ATHENA, A MAN'S GOTTA DO WHAT A MAN'S GOTTA DO!

AND YOU'RE *SOME* MAN, STARBUCK. *MY* MAN.

UH, EURAYLE, DON'T YOU THINK IT'S...UH ...A LITTLE CRAMPED IN HERE?

I THINK IT'S COZY...

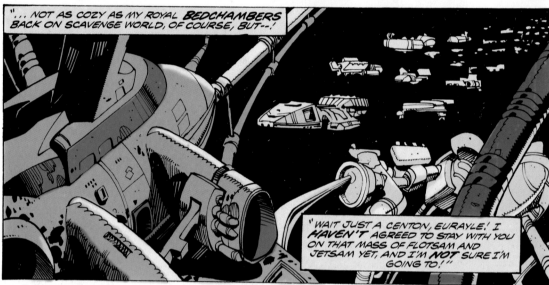

"...NOT AS COZY AS MY ROYAL *BEDCHAMBERS* BACK ON SCAVENGE WORLD, OF COURSE, BUT--!"

"WAIT JUST A *CENTON,* EURAYLE! I *HAVEN'T* AGREED TO STAY WITH YOU ON THAT MASS OF FLOTSAM AND JETSAM YET, AND I'M *NOT* SURE I'M GOING TO!"

"OH, YOU *WILL,* DARLING, IF YOU WANT SCAVENGE WORLD'S HELP IN COMBATING YOUR ENEMIES, THE CYLONS."

"REMEMBER HOW YOUR COMMANDER ADAMA WAS TRAPPED IN THE GALACTICA'S MALFUNCTIONING MEMORY MACHINE?"

"I OFFERED TO HELP FREE HIM, STARBUCK. REMEMBER?"

I CAN SAVE COMMANDER ADAMA. ALL I ASK IN RETURN IS...STARBUCK!

"YOU RECALL HOW YOUR LITTLE FRIEND TRIED TO *STOP* ME...

FORGET IT, EURAYLE! YOU MAY LORD IT OVER THIS RABBLE WORLD OF YOURS BUT YOU *DON'T* OWN US!

WE'RE *NOT* YOUR SLAVES.

ATHENA--

--DON'T *EVER* TOUCH ME AGAIN!

STOP IT, EURAYLE! JUST...JUST STOP YOUR MIND-TRICKS! YOU'RE *KILLING* HER!

SO? SHE DOESN'T MATTER. NOTHING MATTERS EXCEPT *YOU*, STARBUCK. YOU'RE THE ONLY ONE I *CAN'T* CONTROL, LOCK STOCK AND MIND.

YOU FASCINATE ME, STARBUCK, I NEVER THOUGHT *ANY* MAN COULD DO THAT.

MORE FLESH FOR EURAYLE!

FRY HER AGAIN, EURAYLE! WE LIKE TO WATCH HER FRY! OH, WE DO, WE REALLY DO!

SOMETHING WRONG, DARLING? YOU'VE BEEN AWFULLY QUIET. A CUBIT FOR YOUR THOUGHTS.

I WAS JUST WONDERING...

...WHAT HAPPENS WHEN THE FACINATION DIES?

*EURAYLE LOOKS AT HIM AND SMILES, SHRUGGING HER SHOULDERS, A VOICE BUZZES IN STARBUCK'S EAR LIKE A SMALL ELECTRONIC WASP: "ALPHA PATROL CLEARED FOR TOUCHDOWN ON GALACTICA LANDING BAY THREE-NINER."*

*BUT SOMEWHERE IN THE BACK OF HIS MIND AN ALIEN VOICE WHISPERS "FRY HER" OVER AND OVER AGAIN...*

LATER, IN THE SPACIOUS CONFERENCE ROOM OF THE COUNCIL OF TWELVE, THE FLEET'S GOVERNING BODY...

--THAT'S THE SITUATION, GENTLEMEN. EURAYLE IS WILLING TO HELP US, BUT--

--BUT THE PRICE IS TOO HIGH, LIEUTENANT! IT'S OUT-RIGHT BLACKMAIL! WE CAN NOT ASK YOU TO SACRIFICE--

I DISAGREE, COLONEL TIGH!

YOU WOULD, SIRE URI, YOU WOULD!

IT IS CLEAR THIS...UH...WOMAN HAS POWER. I DOUBT WE COULD FIGHT HER. OBVIOUSLY SHE LURED US TO THIS PLACE AND FOR ALL WE KNOW SHE COULD FORCE US TO REMAIN HERE, HELPLESS, UNTIL THE CYLONS FIND US!

YOU'RE A FINE ONE TO TALK, SIRE URI--

IF STARBUCK CAN HELP US, IT IS HIS DUTY TO DO SO. IN THESE TRYING TIMES THE SAFETY OF THE FLEET MUST COME BEFORE ALL ELSE.

LIEUTENANT, LET ME HANDLE THIS BEFORE YOU LOSE YOUR TEMPER.

I'VE HAD JUST ABOUT ALL OF YOU I CAN STOMACH, URI! DON'T THINK I'VE FORGOTTEN YOUR ROLE IN THE LOSS OF OUR AGRO SHIP--

--OR THE NEAR-MUTINY YOU CAUSED THAT TRAPPED COMMANDER ADAMA IN THE MEMORY MACHINE!

THE TIME IS COMING, URI, WHEN YOU'RE GOING TO HAVE TO ANSWER FOR YOUR ACTIONS--

THANKS COLONEL TIGH, BUT URI'S NOT THE PROBLEM HERE NOW, AND MY DECISION IS.

AND YOU'LL HAVE IT WITHIN THE HOUR, BUT RIGHT NOW I'D LIKE TO BE ALONE...

THE YOUNG MAN'S TAKING THIS PRETTY HARD.

WOULDN'T YOU, COUNCILMEMBER PAYNE, IF YOU WERE IN HIS PLACE?

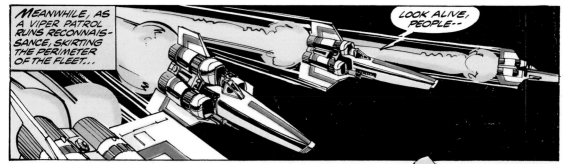

MEANWHILE, AS A VIPER PATROL RUNS RECONNAISSANCE, SKIRTING THE PERIMETER OF THE FLEET...

LOOK ALIVE, PEOPLE--

--WE'RE *NOT* ALONE OUT HERE!

I'VE GOT SOMETHING ON SHIP'S SCANNERS. CO-ORDINATES FOUR-OH-EIGHT, MARK NINER.

CAN'T MAKE A POSITIVE I.D., THOUGH. THIS BLASTED VOID IS STILL PLAYING HAVOC WITH OUR EQUIPMENT.

WE'D BETTER CHECK IT OUT. BUT BE CAREFUL, IT COULD BE--

WITHOUT WARNING, A VIRULENT LASER CUTS THROUGH THE ETERNAL BLACKNESS OF THE VOID, STABBING LIKE A MOLTEN DAGGER, PIERCING THE HEART OF THE LEAD VIPER.

THE EXPLOSION IS SILENT. SO ARE THE PILOT'S DYING SCREAMS...

CYLONS! THEY'VE FOUND US! TAKE EVASIVE ACTION!

WE'VE GOT TO WARN THE GALACTICA!

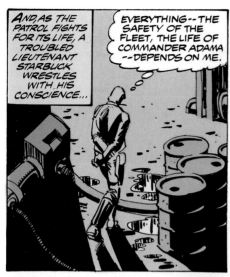

AND, AS THE PATROL FIGHTS FOR ITS LIFE, A TROUBLED LIEUTENANT STARBUCK WRESTLES WITH HIS CONSCIENCE...

EVERYTHING--THE SAFETY OF THE FLEET, THE LIFE OF COMMANDER ADAMA --DEPENDS ON ME.

I KNOW WHAT I HAVE TO DO, BUT--

HEY, BUDDY--

--THOUGHT I'D FIND YOU HERE, FEEL LIKE SOME COMPANY?

I FEEL AWFUL, APOLLO. HOW CAN I GIVE ALL THIS UP? LORD KNOWS I'VE *WANTED* TO, MORE THAN ONCE, BUT THERE'S JUST SOMETHING ABOUT BEING A WARRIOR. IT GETS IN YOUR BLOOD, I GUESS.

JUST LISTEN TO ME. I FINALLY HAVE A CHANCE TO DO SOMETHING *REALLY* IMPORTANT, A CHANCE TO HELP THE FLEET *AND* YOUR FATHER, AND ALL I CAN THINK ABOUT IS MYSELF.

YOU KNOW, CAPTAIN, SOMETIMES I DON'T LIKE ME VERY MUCH AT ALL.

LOOK, STARBUCK, WE'VE GOTTEN OUT OF WORSE SCRAPES BEFORE, WE'LL GET OUT OF THIS ONE, TOO.

I HOPE SO, APOLLO. I DON'T MIND A LITTLE FLING EVERY NOW AND THEN, BUT I'M JUST *NOT* THE SETTLIN' DOWN TYPE.

WHY DO I HAVE TO BE SO DARNED *IRRESIS-TIBLE* TO WOMEN ANYHOW?

AND... ATHENA, WHATEVER HAPPENS, I JUST WANT YOU TO KNOW *YOU'RE* THE ONLY ONE I EVER REALLY LOVED--

OH, STARBUCK, YOU POOR DEAR...

AND SO... SAPHIRE, WHATEVER HAPPENS, I JUST WANT YOU TO KNOW *YOU'RE* THE ONLY ONE I EVER REALLY LOVED--

OH, STARBUCK, YOU POOR DEAR...

AND, SO ON... CASSIOPEA, WHAT-EVER HAPPENS, I JUST WANT YOU TO KNOW *YOU'RE* THE ONLY ONE I EVER REALLY LOVED--

OH, STARBUCK, I BET YOU SAY THAT TO *ALL* THE GIRLS...

THEN...

BREEEEEE

THAT'S A PRIORITY ALERT!

STARBUCK FEELS THE BLOOD-WARRIOR'S BLOOD--POUND IN HIS HEAD AS HE RACES DOWN THE GALACTICA'S GLEAMING CORRIDORS.

AND, EVEN OVER THE SHIP'S BLARING CLAXONS, HE CAN STILL HEAR THE ALIEN VOICE. "FRY HER!" IT SAYS. "FRY HER!" AND THEN IT LAUGHS, LONG AND LOUD AND WITH OBVIOUS GLEE...

GOT TO GET UP TO THE BRIDGE! THERE MUST BE BIG--

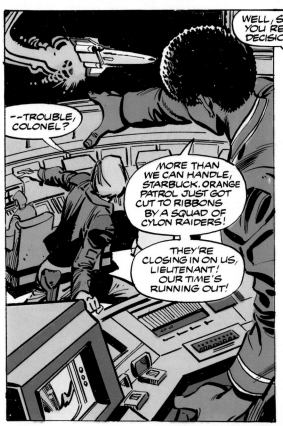

--TROUBLE, COLONEL?

MORE THAN WE CAN HANDLE, STARBUCK. ORANGE PATROL JUST GOT CUT TO RIBBONS BY A SQUAD OF CYLON RAIDERS!

THEY'RE CLOSING IN ON US, LIEUTENANT! OUR TIME'S RUNNING OUT!

WELL, STARBUCK, HAVE YOU REACHED YOUR DECISION?

YOU WIN, EURAYLE. DO WHAT YOU CAN FOR THE FLEET...AND COMMANDER ADAMA...

...AND I'M YOURS...

YOU WON'T BE SORRY, STARBUCK.

THE ALIEN VOICE LAUGHS. "MORE FLESH FOR EURAYLE..."

AND A FEW CENTONS LATER...

GENTLEMEN, OUR SITUATION IS CRITICAL. SCAVENGE WORLD LIES IN THE MAGNETIC CENTER OF THIS VOID.

LIKE A TRUE SARGASSO, EVERY THING IS DRAWN HERE, EVENTUALLY--

--INCLUDING THE CYLONS.

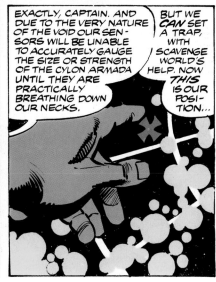

EXACTLY, CAPTAIN. AND DUE TO THE VERY NATURE OF THE VOID OUR SENSORS WILL BE UNABLE TO ACCURATELY GAUGE THE SIZE OR STRENGTH OF THE CYLON ARMADA UNTIL THEY ARE PRACTICALLY BREATHING DOWN OUR NECKS.

BUT WE CAN SET A TRAP, WITH SCAVENGE WORLD'S HELP. NOW THIS IS OUR POSITION...

THAT IS THEIR POSITION, LUCIFER. THE HUMANS APPEAR MIRED IN A LARGE SARGASSO IN THE CENTER OF THE VOID.

OUR SENSORS HAVE FOUND AN APPARENTLY UNGUARDED CORRIDOR THROUGH THE DERELICTS. WE CAN SAFELY ENTER HERE AND SURROUND THE HUMANS. IT IS THE LOGICAL THING TO DO.

YES IT IS, CENTURIAN. BUT THE HUMANS ARE *NOT* A LOGICAL RACE...

OH, MY, YES. THEY *DO* SEEM TRAPPED, DON'T THEY?

POSSIBLY THEY ARE TRYING TO CONCEAL THEM-SELVES AMID THE LIFELESS DEBRIS OF THOUSANDS OF DERELICT SHIPS THAT HAVE, OVER THE MILLINNEA, DRIFTED INTO THE SARGASSO.

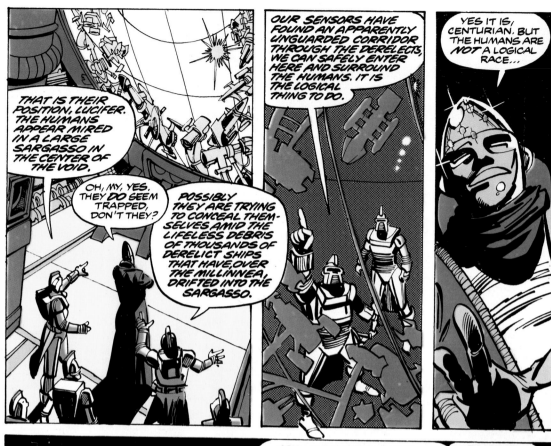

...STILL, I DOUBT THEY ARE EXPECTING A CONCENTRATED ATTACK BY *THREE* BASESHIPS. LAUNCH SQUADRON ONE!

BY YOUR COMMAND...

AND, ON WHAT THE CYLONS CONSIDER THE "LIFELESS" SCAVENGE WORLD...

TELEPATHIC MESSAGE COMING IN FROM EURYALE, OUR QUEEN! HO, BOY! SHE SAYS TO MAN THE GUNS!

AT LAST!

TO ARMS! TO ARMS! FRY THE CYLONS!

SPARE PARTS FOR EVERY-ONE!

AND, ABOARD THE GALACTICA...

READY WHEN YOU ARE, EURAYLE.

I JUST DON'T TRUST ALL THIS ALIEN-HOCUS-POCUS. COMMANDER ADAMA IS TRAPPED IN THE MEMORY MACHINE--

--LOST IN HIS OWN THOUGHTS. IF ANYTHING, GOES WRONG WE COULD *DESTROY* THOSE THOUGHTS, AND ADAMA, FOREVER!

FATHER KNEW THE RISKS INVOLVED, WHEN HE STEPPED INTO THAT MACHINE, STARBUCK. BUT HE DID IT FOR US, FOR THE FLEET.

IF THERE'S A CHANCE, ANY CHANCE AT ALL, TO SAVE HIM WE OWE IT TO HIM TO TAKE IT.

CAPTAIN, IF YOUR FATHER *CAN* BE REACHED, MY MIND-PROBE WILL REACH HIM.

EURAYLE FROWNS IN CONCENTRATION. HER EYES ROLL BACK IN HER HEAD AND SHE SENDS HER THOUGHTS OUT, REACHING FOR A MAN LONG SUBMERGED IN HIS OWN MEMORIES.

AT FIRST THERE IS NOTHING BUT DARKNESS. THEN THE IMAGES COME...

--SO *PEACEFUL* HERE ON CAPRICA, ADAMA, DARLING. I COULD STAY HERE WITH YOU FOREVER.

SO COULD I, ILYA, FOREVER AND EVER, IT'S LIKE A *DREAM* COME TRUE.

DARLING, DID YOU HEAR THAT?

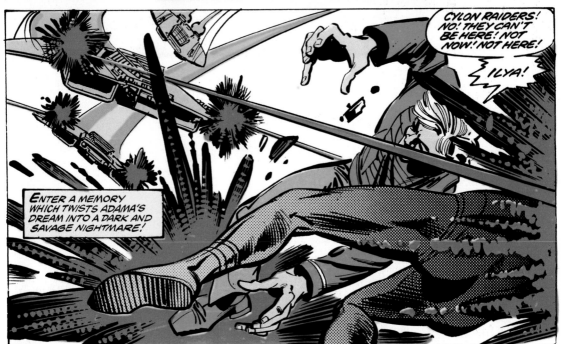

CYLON RAIDERS! NO! THEY CAN'T BE HERE! NOT NOW! NOT HERE!

ILYA!

ENTER A MEMORY WHICH TWISTS ADAMA'S DREAM INTO A DARK AND SAVAGE NIGHTMARE!

MEANWHILE, ON THE BRIDGE...

COLONEL! LONG-RANGE SCANNERS HAVE PICKED UP AN INCOMING FLEET! DEAD AHEAD AND CLOSING FAST!

JUST *ONE* FLEET, ATHENA? YOU'RE SURE OF THAT?

YES, SIR.

THEN WE MAY JUST GET OUT OF THIS YET. THE REST OF OUR SHIPS WILL BE SAFE ON THE FAR SIDE OF SCAVENGE WORLD.

HELMSMAN, PULL THE GALACTICA INTO THE CORRIDOR, BUT *NOT* TOO FAST. GIVE THE CYLONS A TARGET TO LOCK ONTO. LET THEM COME IN AFTER US.

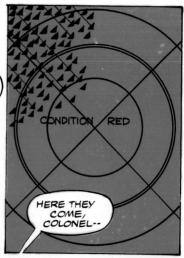

CONDITION RED

HERE THEY COME, COLONEL--

"--AND THEY'RE DROPPING A SENSOR SCREEN! OUR SCANNERS ARE GOING TO HAVE TROUBLE TRACKING THEM!"

CONTINUE ADVANCE. THE HUMANS ARE OFFERING NO RESISTANCE.

THAT'S IT, MAN. STEADY AS SHE GOES.

"THE CYLONS ARE ALMOST ON TOP OF US, COLONEL! THEY'RE OPENING FIRE!"

THE LAMBS ARE ABOUT TO LEAD THE LIONS TO SLAUGHTER!

UNLESS EURAYLE DOUBLE—CROSSES US, COLONEL, IF THAT HAPPENS WE DON'T STAND A CHANCE...

"WHAT'S SCAVENGE WORLD WAITING FOR?"

"LORDS OF KOBOL, WHAT ARE THEY WAITING FOR?"

FRY 'EM!

THE CYLON RAIDERS ARE DESTROYED!

THE CYLON BASE-SHIP MUST BE HOLDING BACK, HIDDEN BEHIND THEIR SENSOR SCREENS! WE'VE GOT TO FORCE THEM TO COME TO US!

KEEP ALL VIPERS ON RED ALERT, READY TO LAUNCH AT MY COMMAND! DAMAGE REPORT, HELMSMAN!

DIRECT HITS ON LEVELS C AND D, COLONEL. STRUCTURAL DAMAGE MODERATE TO HEAVY, BUT--

LEVEL D? YOU'RE SURE OF THAT, MAN? THAT'S WHERE ADAMA IS...

IT'S A MATTER OF LIFE AND DEATH!

...ON LEVEL D!

FRAK! WE'VE GOT TROUBLE, EURAYLE!

OUR LIFE SUPPORT SYSTEMS ARE SHORTING OUT! YOU'VE GOT TO REACH MY FATHER NOW, BEFORE IT'S TOO LATE!

LIFE AND DEATH.

AND THOUGHTS, ALIEN THOUGHTS, POUNDING, PAIN.

THEN ILYA IS GONE-- AND IN HER STEAD...

CYLONS! N-NO, DEAR LORDS, NO! NOT AGAIN...

DRAGGING HIM DOWN, FASTER AND FASTER, TAKING ILYA, SCREAMING, FROM HIM, OUT OF REACH, NO MATTER HOW HARD HE TRIES, HIS MEMORY OF HER FADES...

ADAMMMMAA!

ILYA! NO! I WON'T LEAVE YOU! NOT THIS TIME! NOT EVER AGAIN!

ONCE MORE ADAMA WITNESSES THE DESTRUCTION OF THE HUMAN FLEET BY CYLON TREACHERY!

PRESIDENT ADAR! IT WAS A TRAP! BALTAR PROMISED US PEACE BUT HE LED US INTO A TRAP!

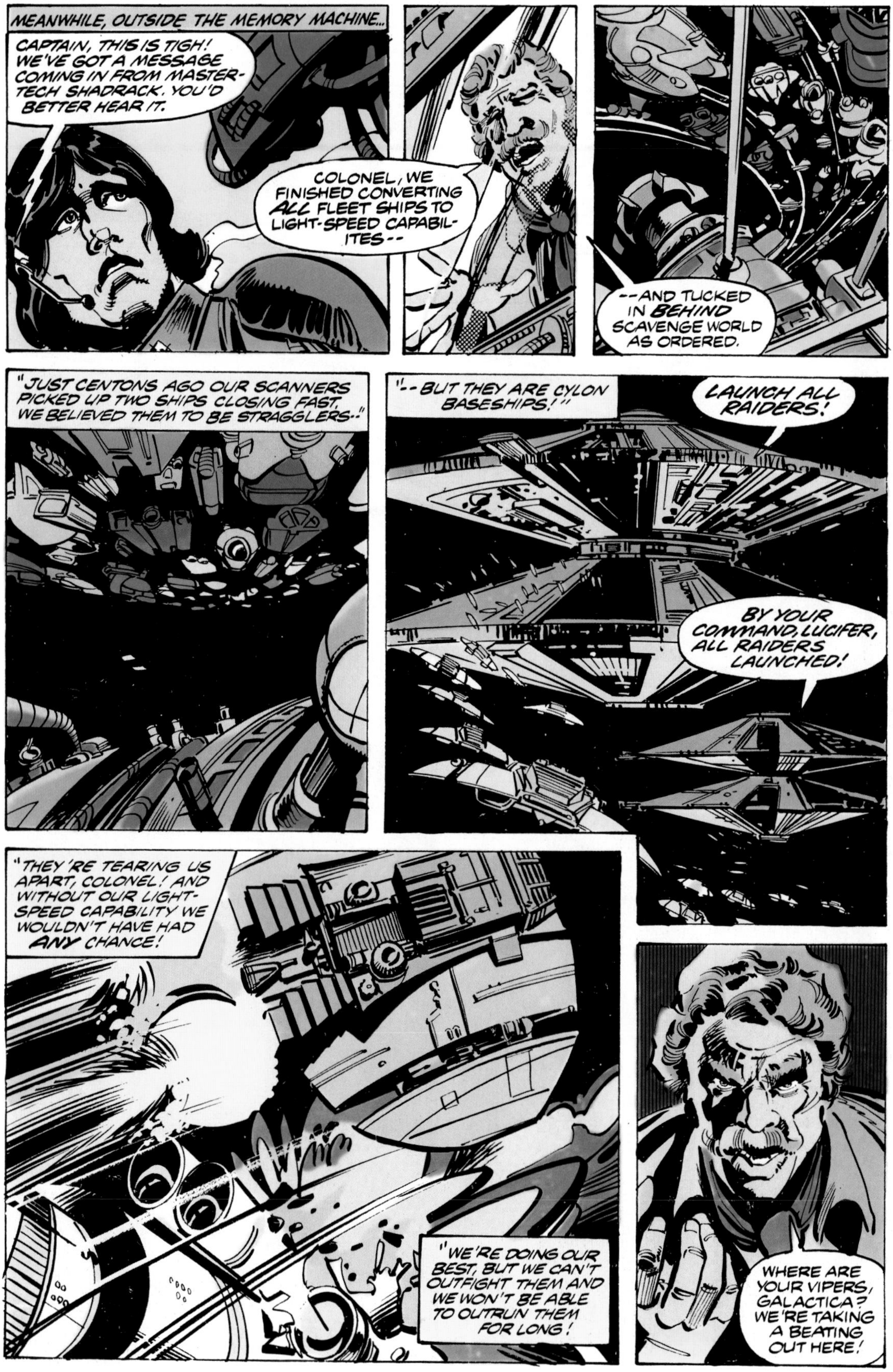
MEANWHILE, OUTSIDE THE MEMORY MACHINE...
CAPTAIN, THIS IS TIGH! WE'VE GOT A MESSAGE COMING IN FROM MASTER-TECH SHADRACK. YOU'D BETTER HEAR IT.
COLONEL, WE FINISHED CONVERTING ALL FLEET SHIPS TO LIGHT-SPEED CAPABIL-ITES--
--AND TUCKED IN BEHIND SCAVENGE WORLD AS ORDERED.
"JUST CENTONS AGO OUR SCANNERS PICKED UP TWO SHIPS CLOSING FAST. WE BELIEVED THEM TO BE STRAGGLERS-"
"--BUT THEY ARE CYLON BASESHIPS!"
LAUNCH ALL RAIDERS!
BY YOUR COMMAND, LUCIFER, ALL RAIDERS LAUNCHED!
"THEY'RE TEARING US APART, COLONEL! AND WITHOUT OUR LIGHT-SPEED CAPABILITY WE WOULDN'T HAVE HAD ANY CHANCE!
"WE'RE DOING OUR BEST, BUT WE CAN'T OUTFIGHT THEM AND WE WON'T BE ABLE TO OUTRUN THEM FOR LONG!
WHERE ARE YOUR VIPERS, GALACTICA? WE'RE TAKING A BEATING OUT HERE!

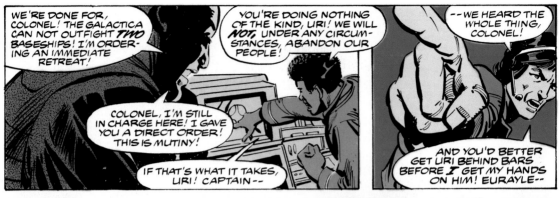

WE'RE DONE FOR, COLONEL! THE GALACTICA CAN NOT OUTFIGHT *TWO* BASESHIPS! I'M ORDERING AN IMMEDIATE RETREAT!

YOU'RE DOING NOTHING OF THE KIND, URI! WE WILL *NOT*, UNDER ANY CIRCUMSTANCES, ABANDON OUR PEOPLE!

--WE HEARD THE WHOLE THING, COLONEL!

COLONEL, I'M STILL IN CHARGE HERE! I GAVE YOU A DIRECT ORDER! THIS IS MUTINY!

IF THAT'S WHAT IT TAKES, URI! CAPTAIN--

AND YOU'D BETTER GET URI BEHIND BARS BEFORE *I* GET MY HANDS ON HIM! EURAYLE--

--WITHOUT LIFE-SUPPORT WE CAN'T STAY IN THIS SECTION MUCH LONGER!

REACH MY FATHER IF YOU CAN! SHOW HIM OUR CRISIS, HERE! WE *NEED* HIM, EURAYLE--

--GIVE IT ALL YOU'VE GOT!

AND WITHIN THE MEMORY MACHINE, ADAMA IS BOMBARDED WITH IMAGES OF HIS PEOPLE'S PLIGHT...

TH-THE GALACTICA! NO! APOLLO! ATHENA! TIGH, OLD FRIEND!

FIGHT BACK! IT'S YOUR ONLY CHANCE! YOU HAVE TO FIGHT! DON'T DIE! NOT LIKE ILYA! NOT LIKE ZAC! YOU'RE ALL I HAVE LEFT!

I WILL NOT LET YOU DIE!

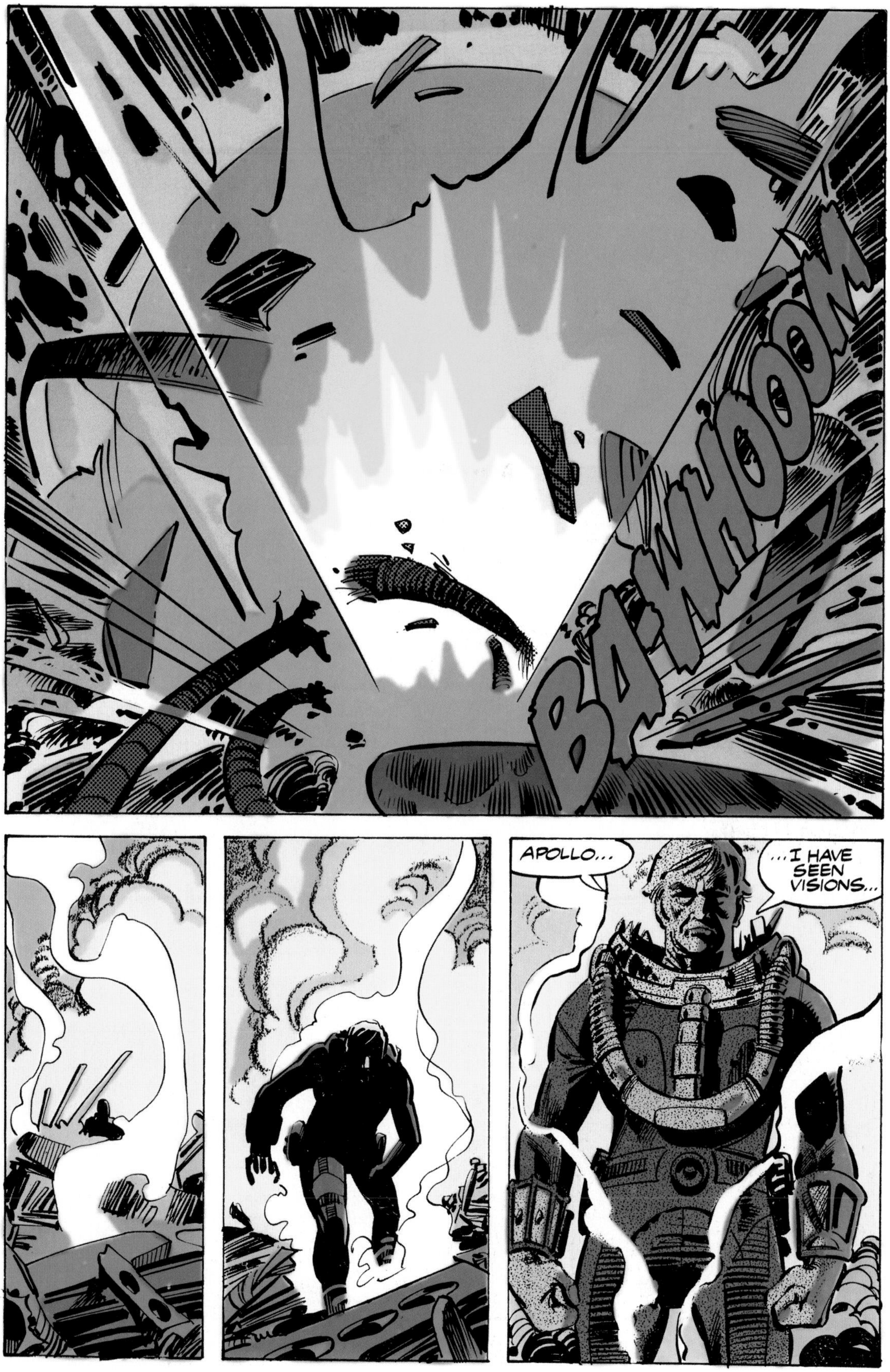
BA-WHOOM
APOLLO...
...I HAVE SEEN VISIONS...

AND, CENTONS LATER...

IT'S ADAMA! HE'S ALIVE!

I KNEW THE OLD MAN'D MAKE IT! HE'S INDESTRUCTABLE!

COMMANDER!

FATHER--! YOU-YOU'RE BACK!

ATHENA--

COMMANDER, I SHARE ATHENA'S JOY, BUT WE HAVE A CRISIS SITUATION HERE! ARE YOU READY TO ASSUME COMMAND OF THE GALACTICA?

I AM, COLONEL!

LAUNCH ALL VIPERS!

THE FLEET MUST BE DEFENDED AT ALL COSTS!

BY YOUR COMMAND, THE GALACTICA HAS LAUNCHED ALL HER VIPERS.

YOU'RE QUITE SURE OF THAT, CENTURIAN?

I AM.

BUT, AS THE VIPERS ROAR ACROSS SCAVENGE WORLD TOWARD THE EMBATTLED FLEET...

THEN WE HAVE THEM! CONTACT OUR *THIRD* BASESHIP. TELL THEM TO EXECUTE PLAN BETA WITHOUT DELAY!

FATHER, WE'RE PICKING UP SOMETHING ON OUR SCANNERS, JUST NOW MOVING OUT OF THE CYLON SENSOR SCREEN! WARBOOK CLASSIFIES IT AS.... BY THE LORDS OF KOBOL ...AS A CYLON BASESHIP!

A *THIRD* BASESHIP? HELMSMAN, HARD ABOUT! FULL EVASIVE TACTICS!

WE *UNDERESTIMATED* THEIR STRENGTH BADLY, APOLLO! THE CYLONS HELD ONE BASESHIP IN RESERVE!

NOW IT'S ON A COLLISION COURSE WITH THE GALACTICA!

IT'S GOING TO *RAM* US AND THERE'S *NOTHING* WE CAN DO TO STOP IT!

NEXT: COLLISION COURSE!

There are those who believe life here began out there, far across the universe, with tribes of humans who may have been the forefathers of the Egyptians. Or the Toltecs. Or the Mayans. Some believe there may yet be brothers of man who even now fight to survive somewhere beyond the heavens!

# Stan Lee PRESENTS: BATTLESTAR GALACTICA™*

Based on the television series Battlestar Galactica™* written and created by Glen Larson.

ROGER MCKENZIE WALT SIMONSON SCRIPT / PLOT / LAYOUTS / KLAUS JANSON FINISHES / ROUSSOS COLORS / COSTANZA LETTERS / ALLEN MILGROM EDITOR / JIM SHOOTER ED.-IN-CHIEF

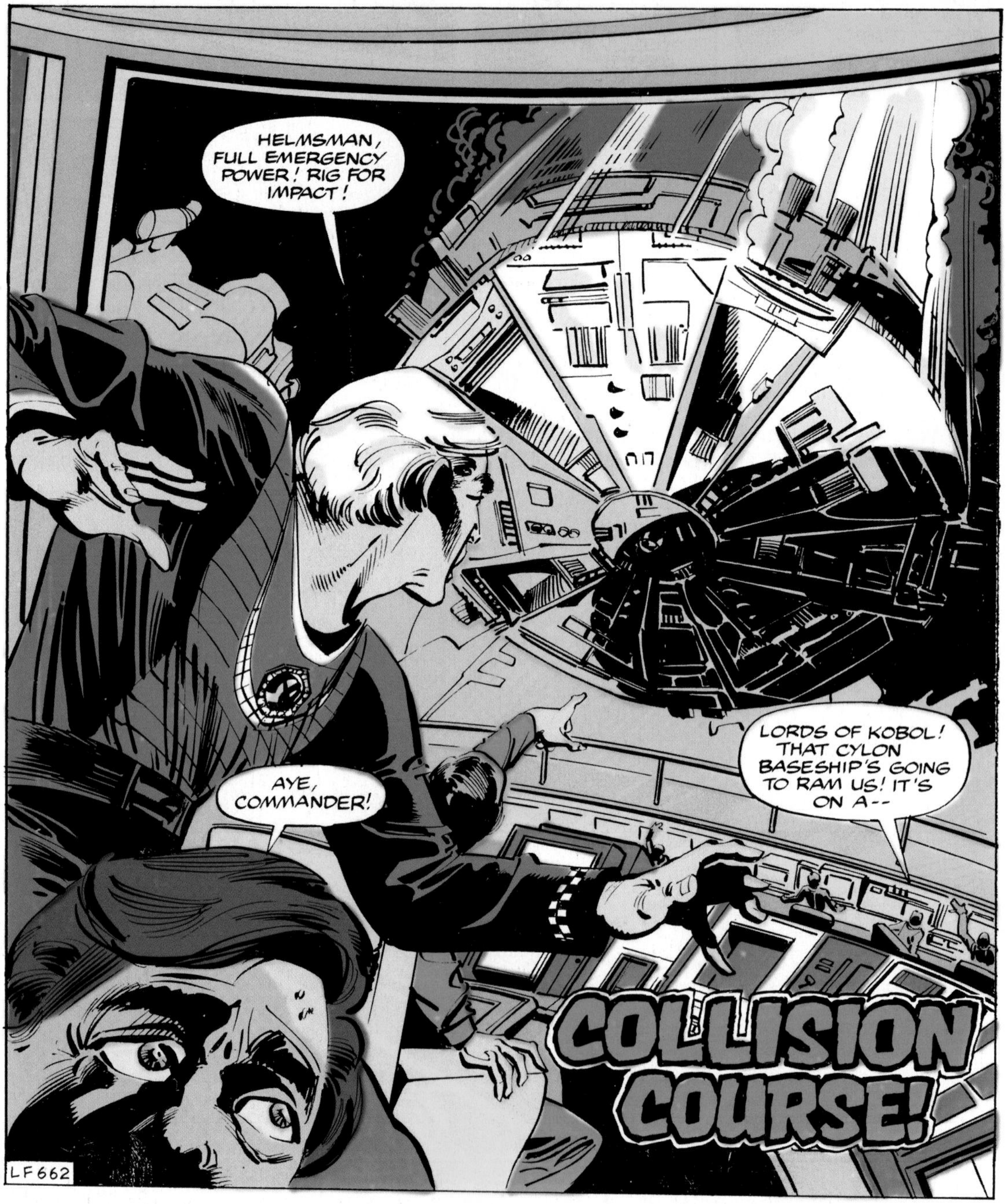
HELMSMAN, FULL EMERGENCY POWER! RIG FOR IMPACT!
LORDS OF KOBOL! THAT CYLON BASESHIP'S GOING TO RAM US! IT'S ON A--
AYE, COMMANDER!
COLLISION COURSE!
LF662

SEVEN THIRTY--?! BUT THAT'LL PUT US *BROAD-SIDE* OF THE BASESHIP! HAS THE COMMANDER LOST HIS MIND? HE'LL GET US ALL KILLED!

LISTEN, MISTER, IF NOT FOR ADAMA WE'D ALL HAVE BEEN KILLED LONG AGO! WE'VE JUST GOTTA PRAY HE'S RIGHT ABOUT THIS! NOW SHUT UP AND OBEY ORDERS, OK?

PATCH ME THROUGH TO QUEEN EURAYLE'S GUNNERS ON SCAVENGE WORLD--

--THEN, ON MY COMMAND, BRING THE GALACTICA AROUND TO HEADING SEVEN-THIRTY-SEVEN, MARK NINE.

AND, ON SCAVENGE WORLD...

HERE COME THE CYLONS! SPARE PARTS FOR EVERYONE TONIGHT!

TRIMMING TO NEW COURSE SEVEN-THIRTY-SEVEN, MARK NINER, COMMANDER.

STEADY AS SHE GOES, HELMSMAN. WE CAN'T HOPE TO OUTRUN THE CYLONS--

--BUT WE CAN TRY TO STOP THEM BEFORE THEY REACH US!

WE'RE IN POSITION, NOW...

FIRE ALL ONBOARD LASERS!

WEAPONS' COMPUTER LOCKED IN AND TRACKING TARGET, COMMANDER. RELAYING COORDIN-ATES TO SCAVENGE WORLD GUN CREWS.

"WHEEOOOHH! YOU HEARD THE GALACTICA, BOYS!"

"FRY THEM SILVER-PLATED BUGGERS! FRY 'EM GOOD!"

NO GO, COMMANDER SCANNER READOUTS INDICATE BASESHIP STILL ON COLLISION COURSE.

FIFTY RADONS AND CLOSING FAST. FORTY FIVE. FORTY...

STATUS REPORT, CENTURIAN.

BY YOUR COMMAND, GARRISON LEADER. DIRECT HITS TO LEVELS THREE THROUGH EIGHTEEN. SUPERSTRUCTURE BUCKLED BUT HOLDING.

WE HAVE LOST SYNC IN UPPER GYROS ALPHA, BETA AND GAMMA. SWITCHING TO RESERVE POWER.

THIRTY RADONS. TWENTY FIVE...

EXTENSIVE DAMAGE TO CENTRAL CORE PYLON, GARRISON LEADER. LOGIC DICTATES IMMEDIATE WITHDRAWAL.

OUR ORDERS ARE QUITE EXPLICIT. CENTURIAN. CRUSH THE GALACTICA AT ALL COSTS. FULL SPEED AHEAD, MAINTAIN PRESENT HEADING.

STILL, IT IS A SHAME WE ARE SO... EXPENDABLE. I RATHER... ENJOYED... FUNCTIONING. OH, WELL...

AT FIRST IT SEEMS COMMANDER ADAMA'S DESPERATE PLAN IS DOOMED TO FAILURE. FOR, ALTHOUGH CAUGHT IN A SAVAGE CROSS-FIRE, THE CYLON JUGGERNAUT STILL HURTLES ON, BEARING DOWN ON THE GALACTICA...

...DETERMINED TO CRUSH THE LAST REMAINING BATTLESTAR JUST AS SURELY AS THEY HAD CRUSHED THE TWELVE COLONIES OF MAN, WITH ONLY THIS HANDFUL OF SURVIVORS MANAGING TO FLEE ACROSS THE HEAVENS.

BUT WITH THE DEADLY MECHANICAL PRECISION OF THEIR KIND, THE CYLONS HAD TRACKED THOSE SURVIVORS HERE, TO THIS DARK VOID SURROUNDING SCAVENGE WORLD. AND NOW--

IT'S WORKING, COMMANDER! THEY'RE COMING APART AT THE SEAMS! SPLITTING AT THE CENTRAL PYLON.

BUT, EVEN RIPPED IN HALF BY ITS FINAL DEATH THROES, THE CYLON BASESHIP SEEMS INTENT ON COMPLETING ITS MURDEROUS MISSION.

RAINING TONS OF BLACKENED DEBRIS PAST THE GALACTICA, IT GOUGES HUGE CHUNKS FROM HER HULL...

...BEFORE FINALLY SLAMMING ROUGHLY INTO THE METALLIC SURFACE OF SCAVENGE WORLD.

THE FALL OF THE BASESHIP DOES NOT GO UNNOTICED BY THE INHABITANTS OF SCAVENGE WORLD, AS WELDERS AND MECHANICS AND ROGUES AND BUILDERS, HUNDREDS STRONG, SCURRY TO THE CRASH SITE...

OH, HAPPY DAY! OH GLORIOUS MORNING! SPARE PARTS FOR SCAVENGE WORLD!

I GET THE CHROME!

NO! ME! ME!

WHILE, ABOARD THE CRIPPLED GALACTICA...

HELMSMAN, ALL ENGINES DEAD STOP! REPAIR CREWS TO SECTOR FOUR, STERN STABILIZER TWO... ON THE DOUBLE!

"FATHER, WE JUST CAN'T SIT HERE LICKING OUR WOUNDS! THE FLEET IS UNDER DIRECT ATTACK! WE'VE GOT TO REACH THEM BEFORE THE CYLONS TEAR THEM TO PIECES"

"DO YOU THINK I DON'T KNOW THAT, APOLLO? BUT UNLESS WE REPAIR THE DAMAGE TO THE GALACTICA'S HULL WE MAY NEVER REACH THEM!"

MAY THE LORDS OF KOBOL HAVE MERCY, THERE'S NOTHING ELSE WE CAN DO.

THERE'S SOMETHING I CAN DO, FATHER. I CAN REJOIN THE FLEET IN MY VIPER. THEY'LL NEED EVERY WARRIOR THEY CAN GET.

SPLENDID, CAPTAIN...

...AND SINCE I HAVE FULFILLED MY PART OF OUR... AH... AGREEMENT AND FREED YOUR FATHER FROM THE MEMORY MACHINE* YOU MAY NOW ESCORT LIEUTENANT STARBUCK AND I BACK TO SCAVENGE WORLD.

THAT'S OUT OF THE QUESTION, EURAYLE! STARBUCK BELONGS HERE!

NO, HE BELONGS TO ME, ADAMA. A DEAL'S A DEAL...

* IF YOU MISSED LAST ISSUE YOU'LL JUST HAVE TO TAKE OUR WORD FOR IT--AL.

A FEW CENTONS LATER...

SOME DEAL--! BLACKMAIL'S MORE LIKE IT! STARBUCK, YOU CAN'T GO THROUGH WITH THIS!

I DON'T HAVE ANY CHOICE, APOLLO. FOR WHATEVER REASON, I'M IMMUNE TO EURAYLE'S MIND-CONTROLLING POWERS...

...BUT SHE COULD WREAK HAVOC ON THE REST OF THE FLEET WITH A SINGLE THOUGHT!

I DON'T WANT THAT ON MY CONSCIENCE, APOLLO...

EVEN IF IT MEANS SPENDING THE REST OF MY LIFE ON A CHUNK OF SPACE DEBRIS SOMEWHERE IN THE MIDDLE OF NOWHERE...

GRIMLY THE TWO FRIENDS PART, THEIR FINAL WORDS LOST IN THE BACKLASH OF ENGINES ROARING TO LIFE...

...AS, FIRST APOLLO'S SLEEK VIPER, AND THEN QUEEN EURAYLE'S MAKESHIFT FLAGSHIP, ROAR FROM THE GALACTICA.

WELL, WELL--! STARBUCK, YOUR FRIENDS CERTAINLY HATED TO SEE YOU GO!

CHEER UP, LOVER, YOU'RE GOING TO BE A KING!

KING OF SCAVENGE WORLD. MY KING.

SWELL.

AND SPEAKING OF SCAVENGE WORLD, HERE WE ARE,

HERE WE GO! BLUE SQUADRON!

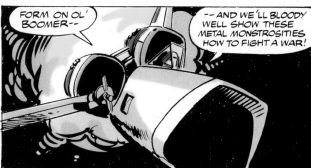

FORM ON OL' BOOMER--

-- AND WE'LL BLOODY WELL SHOW THESE METAL MONSTROSITIES HOW TO FIGHT A WAR!

AFTER ALL, WE CAN'T BE OUTNUMBERED MORE THAN TEN TO ONE, RIGHT?

BY YOUR COMMAND, LUCIFER. COMPUTER ESTIMATES INDICATE THAT DESPITE HEAVY LOSSES WE STILL OUTNUMBER THE HUMANS TWENTY-TO-ONE.

AND I'M GLAD I DECIDED TO DIRECT THAT ANNIHILATION FIRST HAND! THIS IS GREAT FUN!

"ADVENTURE! EXCITEMENT! THE THRILL OF THE HUNT! THE -- OH, NEVER MIND, CENTURIAN! HONESTLY, YOU B-2 UNITS ARE SO DREADFULLY DULL YOU MAKE ME MISS THE HUMAN TRAITOR, BALTAR! AT LEAST HE HAD A SENSE OF HUMOR!"

FUN? I DO NOT UNDERSTAND.

EXCELLENT, CENTURIAN, EXCELLENT! IT'S ONLY A MATTER OF TIME NOW BEFORE WE COMPLETE OUR PRIME FUNCTION -- TOTAL ANNIHILATION OF THE HUMAN RACE!

"STILL, I WONDER WHY THERE'S BEEN NO FURTHER WORD FROM OUR THIRD BASESHIP! IS IT POSSIBLE THE GALACTICA ACTUALLY MANAGED TO ESCAPE --?"

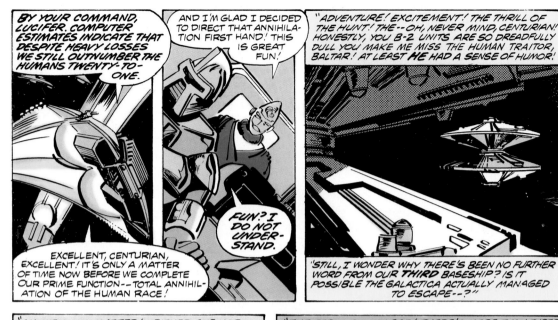

"AH, WELL, NO MATTER! NEITHER SHE NOR THE SO-CALLED FLEET SHE CHAMPIONS WILL ESCAPE THE COMBINED MIGHT OF OUR TWO REMAINING BASESHIPS! WE CAN'T LOSE, CENTURIAN!"

"AND THAT IS THE MEANING OF... FUN... LUCIFER?"

"CENTURIAN, THERE'S HOPE FOR YOU YET!"

"THE JERI-- OH, MY GOD! THERE'S MORE THAN THREE HUNDRED PEOPLE REGISTERED ABOARD THAT OLD TUG!

"DEPLOY ALL AVAILABLE SHUTTLES, SERGEANT! WE'VE GOT TO EVACUATE THAT SHIP BEFORE --"

THERE'S NO HOPE FOR US, SHADRACK! NOT WITHOUT THE GALACTICA! WHERE IS SHE?

"IT'S TOO LATE, SHADRACK. WE-- WE'VE LOST HER..."

I WISH I KNEW, SERGEANT, I --

-- DISTRESS CALL COMING IN FROM THE GARBAGE SCOW JERICO, SIR! SHE'S UNDER DIRECT ATTACK!

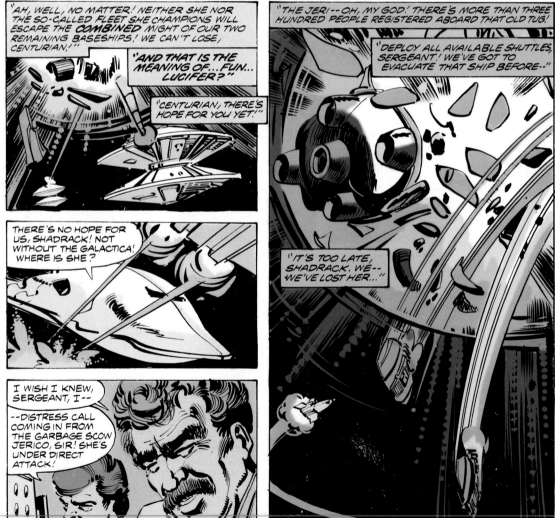

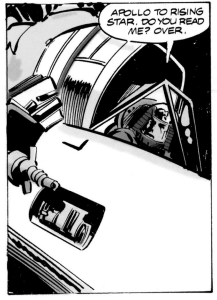

APOLLO TO RISING STAR. DO YOU READ ME? OVER.

PATCH ME THROUGH TO HIM, SERGEANT!

YOU'RE ON AUDIO, SHADRACK, GO AHEAD.

APOLLO! WHERE'S THE GALACTICA, MAN? WE'RE GETTING TORN APART OUT HERE!

THE GALACTICA'S NOT IN MUCH BETTER SHAPE. SHE WAS NEARLY RAMMED BY--

OF COURSE! THAT'S IT, SHADRACK, LISTEN! I'VE GOT AN IDEA...

SHADRACK LISTENS...

...BUT HE DOESN'T BELIEVE WHAT HE HEARS...

APOLLO, THAT'S INSANE! YOU CAN'T JUST--

WHAT? A DIRECT ORDER? YES, SIR...I'LL... I'LL DO WHAT I CAN. AND CAPTAIN, GOOD LUCK...

AND SO...

MOVE OUT, WARRIORS! MASTER-TECH SHADRACK SAID WE WERE TO RENDEZVOUS WITH APOLLO...

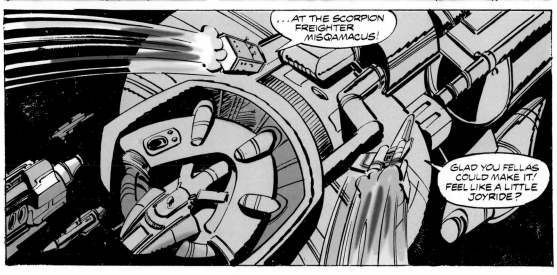

...AT THE SCORPION FREIGHTER MISQAMACUS!

GLAD YOU FELLAS COULD MAKE IT! FEEL LIKE A LITTLE JOYRIDE?

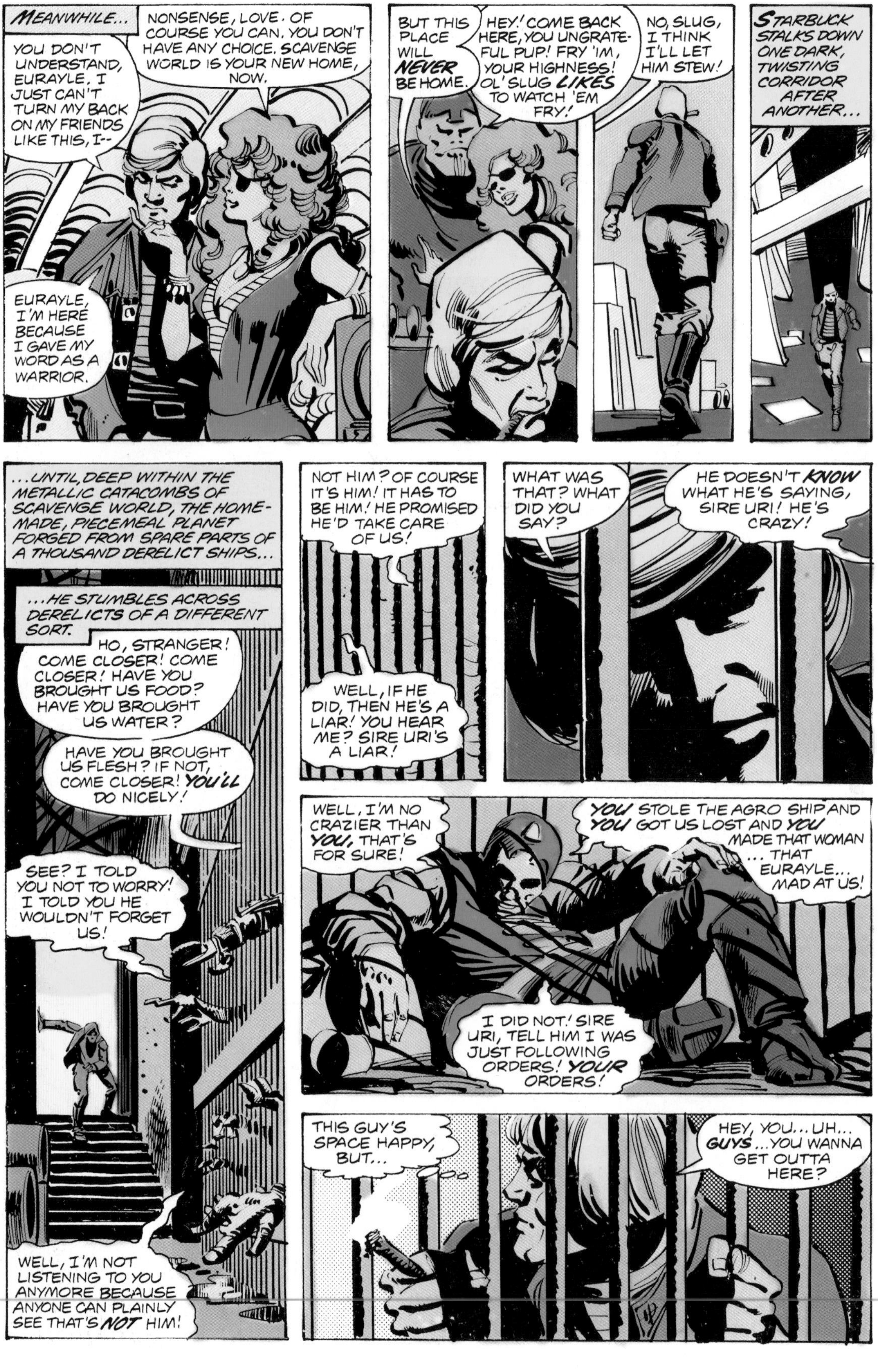
MEANWHILE...
YOU DON'T UNDERSTAND, EURAYLE. I JUST CAN'T TURN MY BACK ON MY FRIENDS LIKE THIS, I--
NONSENSE, LOVE. OF COURSE YOU CAN. YOU DON'T HAVE ANY CHOICE. SCAVENGE WORLD IS YOUR NEW HOME, NOW.
EURAYLE, I'M HERE BECAUSE I GAVE MY WORD AS A WARRIOR.
BUT THIS PLACE WILL NEVER BE HOME.
HEY! COME BACK HERE, YOU UNGRATEFUL PUP! FRY 'IM, YOUR HIGHNESS! OL' SLUG LIKES TO WATCH 'EM FRY!
NO, SLUG, I THINK I'LL LET HIM STEW!
STARBUCK STALKS DOWN ONE DARK, TWISTING CORRIDOR AFTER ANOTHER...
...UNTIL, DEEP WITHIN THE METALLIC CATACOMBS OF SCAVENGE WORLD, THE HOME-MADE, PIECEMEAL PLANET FORGED FROM SPARE PARTS OF A THOUSAND DERELICT SHIPS...
...HE STUMBLES ACROSS DERELICTS OF A DIFFERENT SORT.
HO, STRANGER! COME CLOSER! COME CLOSER! HAVE YOU BROUGHT US FOOD? HAVE YOU BROUGHT US WATER?
HAVE YOU BROUGHT US FLESH? IF NOT, COME CLOSER! YOU'LL DO NICELY!
SEE? I TOLD YOU NOT TO WORRY! I TOLD YOU HE WOULDN'T FORGET US!
WELL, I'M NOT LISTENING TO YOU ANYMORE BECAUSE ANYONE CAN PLAINLY SEE THAT'S NOT HIM!
NOT HIM? OF COURSE IT'S HIM! IT HAS TO BE HIM! HE PROMISED HE'D TAKE CARE OF US!
WELL, IF HE DID, THEN HE'S A LIAR! YOU HEAR ME? SIRE URI'S A LIAR!
WHAT WAS THAT? WHAT DID YOU SAY?
HE DOESN'T KNOW WHAT HE'S SAYING, SIRE URI! HE'S CRAZY!
WELL, I'M NO CRAZIER THAN YOU, THAT'S FOR SURE!
YOU STOLE THE AGRO SHIP AND YOU GOT US LOST AND YOU MADE THAT WOMAN... THAT EURAYLE... MAD AT US!
I DID NOT! SIRE URI, TELL HIM I WAS JUST FOLLOWING ORDERS! YOUR ORDERS!
THIS GUY'S SPACE HAPPY, BUT...
HEY, YOU... UH... GUYS... YOU WANNA GET OUTTA HERE?

MEANWHILE, IN THE DARK, STARLESS VOID AROUND SCAVENGE WORLD, THE GALACTICA, HER DAMAGED HULL TEMPORARILY REPAIRED, CONFRONTS MADNESS OF ANOTHER SORT ENTIRELY.

THE MADNESS OF WAR...

AHEAD FLANK SPEED, HELMSMAN! ALL LASER BATTERIES FIRE AT WILL!

BY YOUR COMMAND, LUCIFER THE GALACTICA HAS JUST MOVED INTO SCANNER RANGE.

SO, THE BATTLESTAR STILL SURVIVES! I SUSPECTED AS MUCH...

...BUT I DON'T SUSPECT SHE'LL SURVIVE MUCH LONGER! HER TIME IS RUNNING OUT!

HURRY IT UP, MAN! OUR TIME'S RUNNING OUT!

DOIN' MY BEST, CAPTAIN APOLLO! THE LAST OF THE MISQUMA-CUS' INHABITANTS HAVE JUST SHUTTLED OFF BOARD...

...AND I'M SETTING THE CHARGES NOW. BUT I DON'T KNOW HOW WE'RE GONNA DETONATE 'EM.

WE AREN'T GOING TO, SERGEANT. STAND BY.

--BECAUSE WE'RE MOVING OUT!

THE ANCIENT FREIGHTER GROANS IN PROTEST...

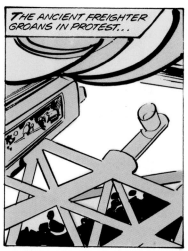

...HER AGED ENGINES SPUTTERING TO LIFE ONE FINAL TIME...

...AS SHE RUMBLES PAST THE BARREN, METALLIC SURFACE OF SCAVENGE WORLD, SLOWLY BUT SURELY PICKING UP SPEED...

SHE MAY NOT LOOK LIKE MUCH, CAP'N, BUT THIS OLD TUB'S HOLDIN' TOGETHER JUST FINE!

IT'S HER LAST MISSION, ENSIGN. LET'S MAKE IT COUNT FOR SOMETHING.

THIS IS THE MISQUAMACUS! ANYONE READ ME? OVER.

FATHER, WE'RE PICKING UP A STRANGE TRANSMISSION. I THINK IT'S APOLLO, BUT--

PATCH ME THROUGH TO HIM, ATHENA.

WE READ YOU LOUD AND CLEAR, MISQUAMACUS! APOLLO, WHAT--

GOOD TO SEE YOU BACK IN ACTION, GALACTICA! YOU'RE A SIGHT FOR SORE EYES!

THERE'S NO TIME TO EXPLAIN, FATHER, BUT WE'LL NEED AN ESCORT...

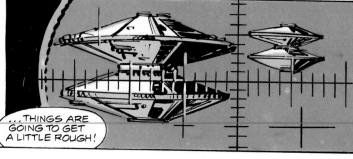

...THINGS ARE GOING TO GET A LITTLE ROUGH!

BY YOUR COMMAND. THE GALACTICA HAS COME ABOUT AND WOULD SEEM TO BE ON A COLLISION COURSE WITH OUR BASESHIPS.

WHAT?! BY THE GREAT MACHINE, IS THERE NO LIMIT TO HUMAN ILLOGIC?

ALL RAIDERS CONVERGE ON THE BATTLESTAR! DESTROY IT, ONCE AND FOR ALL!

BY YOUR COMMAND. COMMENCING ATTACK.

HOLD YOUR PRESENT COURSE, HELMSMAN! WE MUST PROTECT THE MISQUAMACUS AT ALL COSTS!

"TEN RADONS AND CLOSING, CAP'N."

STEADY AS SHE GOES, HELMSMAN!

"FIVE RADONS AND STILL CLOSING."

THANKS FOR A JOB WELL DONE, GALACTICA...

--BUT FROM HERE ON OUT, WE'RE ON OUR OWN.!

FOUR RADONS AND-- *FRAK!*

SCANNERS HAVE A CYLON RAIDER AT NINE O'CLOCK AND CLOSING AT ATTACK SPEED!

NO--! IT'S TOO SOON! WE'RE NOT CLOSE ENOUGH TO THE BASESHIPS, YET!

ENSIGN, WE WILL FLY THE ESCAPE CAPSULE OUT OF HERE--

-- WE'RE GOING TO HAVE TO GIVE THE CYLONS A NICE, BIG TARGET AND DIVERT THEIR ATTENTION FROM THE *MISQUAMACUS* IF WE CAN!

BUT, AS THE RAIDER CLOSES IN MERCILESS-LY, EXPECTING AN EASY KILL--

--THE HUNTERS SUDDENLY FIND THEMSELVES THE HUNTED! AS THE CYLON FIGHTER IS BLASTED TO BITS!

YAHOOO--! GOT 'EM!

I KNEW YOU SPACE JOCKIES COULDN'T FIGHT A DECENT WAR WITHOUT OL' STARBUCK!

UNIDENTIFIED SPACECRAFT WITHIN CYLON DEFENSE PERIMETERS! ALL BATTERIES OPEN FIRE.

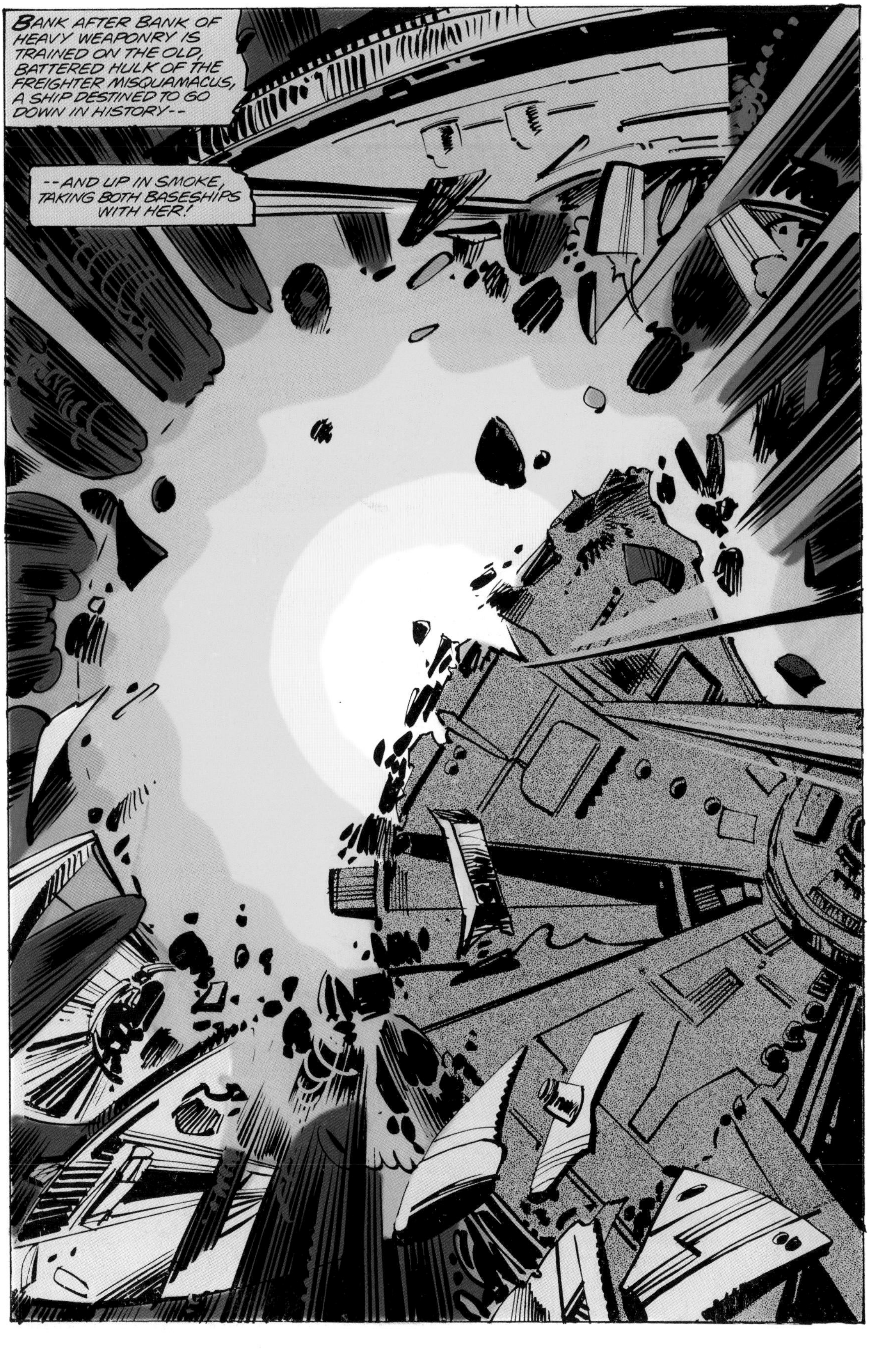
BANK AFTER BANK OF HEAVY WEAPONRY IS TRAINED ON THE OLD, BATTERED HULK OF THE FREIGHTER MISQUAMACUS, A SHIP DESTINED TO GO DOWN IN HISTORY--
--AND UP IN SMOKE, TAKING BOTH BASESHIPS WITH HER!

APOLLO!

AND HER FUNERAL PYRE LIGHTS THE VOID FOR THE FIRST TIME IN MILLENIA...

HOLD ON--! WE'RE CAUGHT IN THE BACKLASH OF THE EXPLOSION! OUR CAPSULE'S COMING APART AT THE SEAMS!

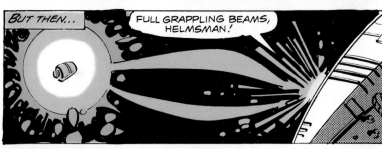

BUT THEN...

FULL GRAPPLING BEAMS, HELMSMAN!

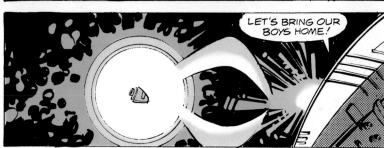

LET'S BRING OUR BOYS HOME!

DOES THAT GO FOR ME, TOO, COMMANDER?

IT'S A LONG STORY, COMMANDER. LET'S JUST SAY I'VE GOT SOMEONE WITH ME WHO'S... BESIDE HIMSELF TO SEE YOU!

BUT, EVEN AS STARBUCK DOCKS HIS COMMANDEERED SHIP WITH THE GALACTICA, A CERTAIN CYLON RAIDER SLIPS UNOBSERVED INTO THE TRACKLESS VOID...

STARBUCK?! WHAT IN THE NAME OF KOBOL--

THE HUMAN DESTROYED ALL THREE OF OUR BASESHIPS, LUCIFER. THIS IS NOT FUN.

NO, CENTURIAN, THIS... IS... NOT... FUN...

DISORGANIZED AND LEADERLESS, THE REMNANTS OF THE ONCE-AWESOME CYLON TASK FORCE ARE QUICKLY ROUTED.

AND, ALTHOUGH IT WILL TAKE MANY LONG DAYS TO ACCURATELY DETERMINE THE NUMBER OF SHIPS AND LIVES LOST, ONE THING IS CERTAIN EVEN IN THE GRIM AFTERMATH OF THE BATTLE OF SCAVENGE WORLD...

...THE RAGTAG COLONIAL FLEET STILL STANDS!

AND, ON THE BRIDGE OF THE GALACTICA...

CONVOY FROM SCAVENGE WORLD REQUESTING... NO, DEMANDING... LANDING CLEARANCE, COMMANDER.

DEMANDING? THAT *HAS* TO BE EURAYLE.

AND SHE HAS TO KNOW STARBUCK IS MISSING.

YEAH, WELL, YOU KNOW HOW IT IS, COMMANDER. I MISSED THE CHOW.

AND SPEAKING OF FOOD, I RAN ACROSS SOMEONE I THOUGHT YOU'D LIKE TO MEET, COMMANDER...THE MAN WHO STOLE OUR AGRO SHIP AND GOT US INTO THIS IN THE FIRST PLACE.

WE DIDN'T STEAL ANYTHING! WE WERE JUST FOLLOWING ORDERS!

SIRE URI'S ORDERS!

HOLD IT RIGHT THERE, URI!

EH--?

SURELY, OLD FRIEND, YOU DON'T BELIEVE THE DESPERATE PROTESTATIONS OF A...A MADMAN?

URI, I BELIEVE YOU HAD BETTER CHOOSE *YOUR* WORDS CAREFULLY! I'M PLACING YOU UNDER ARREST!

AND, AS GUARDS ESCORT A PROTESTING SIRE URI AWAY--

...AN ARMED ENVOY, HEADED BY QUEEN EURAYLE, ESCORTS THE MISSING AGRO SHIP BACK TO THE COLONIAL FLEET.

AND THEN...

THERE HE IS! COMMANDER... CAPTAIN... STAND ASIDE--

-- STARBUCK IS MINE!

STARBUCK, I DON'T KNOW HOW YOU MAN-AGED TO ESCAPE SCAVENGE WORLD, AND FRANKLY, I DON'T CARE.

BUT IT WILL NOT HAPPEN AGAIN!

ADAMA, I HAVE RETURNED YOUR AGRO SHIP AND MY GUIDES WILL LEAD YOU OUT OF THE VOID. THE PACT IS FULFILLED.

AHEAD FLANK SPEED, HELMSMAN.

YOU HAVE YOUR PRECIOUS FREEDOM AND I HAVE STARBUCK.

EURAYLE, BE RESONABLE. YOU CAN'T ASK STARBUCK TO--

THE MATTER IS CLOSED, COMMANDER. STARBUCK WILL REMAIN WITH ME ON SCAVENGE WORLD--

--TO HIS DYING DAY!

NEXT ISSUE: TRIAL and ERROR!